The family table

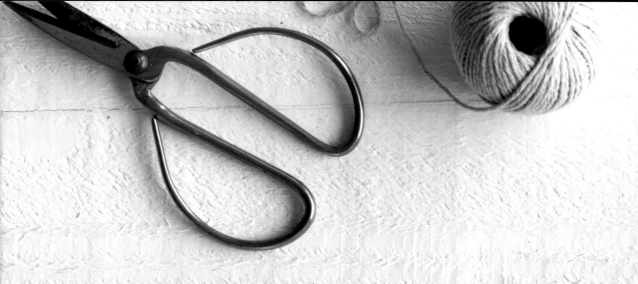

Published in 2015 by Bounty Books based on materials licensed to it by Bauer Media Books, Australia

MEDIA GROUP

Bauer Media Books are published by
Bauer Media Pty Limited, 54 Park St, Sydney;
GPO Box 4088, Sydney, NSW 2001, Australia.
phone +61 2 9282 8618; fax +61 2 9126 3702
www.awwcookbooks.com.au

BAUER MEDIA BOOKS
Publisher Jo Runciman
Editorial & food director Pamela Clark
Director of sales, marketing & rights Brian Cearnes
Creative director Hieu Chi Nguyen
Designer Jeannel Cunanan
Junior editor Amy Bayliss
Food concept director Sophia Young
Food editor Emma Braz
Operations manager David Scotto

Printed in China with 1010 Printing Asia Limited

Published and distributed in the United Kingdom by
Bounty Books, a division of
Octopus Publishing Group Ltd

Carmelite House
50 Victoria Embankment
London, EC4Y 0DZ
United Kingdom
info@octopus-publishing.co.uk;
www.octopusbooks.co.uk

International foreign language rights,
Brian Cearnes, Bauer Media Books
bcearnes@bauer-media.com.au

A catalogue record for this book is available from the British Library.
ISBN: 978-0-7537-2992-2
© Bauer Media Pty Limited 2015
ABN 18 053 273 546

THE AUSTRALIAN

Women's Weekly

The family table

Bounty
BOOKS

CONTENTS

FAST

WHEN THE HUSTLE AND
BUSTLE OF THE WEEK GETS
A LITTLE TOO MUCH, THE KEY
IS TO MAKE FAMILY FOOD
WITH MINIMUM FUSS.
TAKE ADVANTAGE OF THESE
RECIPES THAT ARE READY IN
30 MINUTES OR UNDER.

PALM SUGAR IS USUALLY SOLD IN ROCK-HARD CAKES THAT NEED TO BE GRATED. YOU CAN USE BROWN SUGAR IF IT'S NOT AVAILABLE.

PORK LARB WITH BROCCOLINI AND NOODLES

PREP + COOK TIME 25 MINUTES ◆ SERVES 4

1 tablespoon peanut oil

2 cloves garlic, crushed

600g (1¼ pounds) minced (ground) pork

⅓ cup (90g) grated palm sugar

2 tablespoons fish sauce

4 fresh kaffir lime leaves, sliced finely

½ cup (40g) fried shallots

⅓ cup (45g) roasted unsalted peanuts

350g (11 ounces) broccolini, trimmed, halved lengthways

250g (8 ounces) fresh egg noodles

1 tablespoon lime juice

1 cup loosely packed fresh coriander (cilantro) leaves

1 fresh long red chilli, sliced thinly

2 tablespoons coarsely chopped roasted unsalted peanuts

1 Heat oil in a wok over high heat; stir-fry garlic and pork for 5 minutes or until pork is browned.

2 Add sugar, sauce, lime leaves, shallots and peanuts to wok. Reduce heat to low; stir-fry for 2 minutes or until mixture is slightly dry and sticky.

3 Meanwhile, boil, steam or microwave broccolini; drain well. Cook noodles following packet directions.

4 Remove larb from heat; add juice, three-quarters of the coriander, noodles and broccolini.

5 Serve larb scattered with remaining coriander, chilli and chopped peanuts.

TEST KITCHEN NOTES

FRIED SHALLOTS ARE AVAILABLE FROM ASIAN GROCERY STORES. LEFTOVER LARB CAN BE SERVED COLD IN LETTUCE LEAVES FOR AN EASY LUNCH. SUBSTITUTE BROCCOLI FOR BROCCOLINI.

PEPPERED FILLET STEAKS WITH CREAMY BOURBON SAUCE

PREP + COOK TIME 20 MINUTES ♦ SERVES 4

4 x 125g (4 ounces) beef fillet steaks

2 teaspoons cracked black pepper

2 tablespoons olive oil

6 shallots (150g), sliced thinly

1 clove garlic, crushed

⅓ cup (80ml) bourbon

¼ cup (60ml) beef stock

2 teaspoons dijon mustard

300ml pouring cream

1 Rub both sides of beef with pepper. Heat half the oil in a large frying pan over medium-high heat; cook beef for 3 minutes each side or until cooked as desired. Remove from pan; cover to keep warm.

2 Heat remaining oil in same pan; cook shallots and garlic, stirring, until shallots soften. Add bourbon; stir until mixture simmers and starts to thicken. Stir in stock, mustard and cream; bring to the boil. Reduce heat; simmer, uncovered, for 5 minutes or until sauce thickens slightly.

3 Serve beef drizzled with sauce.

TEST KITCHEN NOTES

FOR MEDIUM, COOK FILLETS ABOUT 3 MINUTES EACH SIDE; IF YOU LIKE YOUR STEAK WELL DONE, COOK A FURTHER MINUTE ON EACH SIDE, OR FOR A RARER STEAK REDUCE COOKING TIME TO 1 MINUTE EACH SIDE. REST THE STEAK, COVERED LOOSELY WITH FOIL, TO ALLOW THE MEAT TO RELAX AND DISTRIBUTE THE JUICES THROUGH THE STEAK.

BOURBON

IS A TYPE OF
AMERICAN WHISKEY
DISTILLED MAINLY
FROM CORN.

**SERVING
SUGGESTION**

FRIED POTATOES AND
STEAMED GREEN
ASPARAGUS.

TOMATO AND CHILLI PASTA

PREP + COOK TIME 20 MINUTES ◆ SERVES 4

375g (12 ounces) penne pasta

1 fresh small red thai (serrano) chilli, chopped finely

3 medium ripe tomatoes (450g), chopped coarsely

¾ cup coarsely chopped fresh flat-leaf parsley

1 Cook pasta in a large saucepan of boiling water until tender; drain.

2 Meanwhile, heat an oiled large frying pan; cook chilli, stirring, for 1 minute or until fragrant. Stir in tomato and parsley; remove from heat.

3 Add sauce mixture to pasta; toss to combine. Sprinkle with grated parmesan to serve, if you like.

TEST KITCHEN NOTES

THIS IS A GREAT BASIC PASTA SAUCE; ADD DRAINED AND FLAKED CANNED TUNA, DRAINED ANTIPASTO MIX OR SLICES OF SALAMI FOR QUICK VARIATIONS.

STIR-FRIED LAMB IN BLACK BEAN SAUCE

PREP + COOK TIME 30 MINUTES ◆ SERVES 4

⅔ cup (130g) white long-grain rice

600g (1¼ pounds) lamb strips

1 teaspoon chinese five-spice powder

2 teaspoons sesame oil

2 tablespoons peanut oil

2 cloves garlic, crushed

1 teaspoon finely grated fresh ginger

1 medium brown onion (150g), sliced thinly

1 small red capsicum (bell pepper) (150g), sliced thinly

1 small yellow capsicum (bell pepper) (150g), sliced thinly

500g (1 pound) choy sum, chopped coarsely

1 teaspoon cornflour (cornstarch)

½ cup (125ml) chicken stock

1 tablespoon soy sauce

2 tablespoons black bean sauce

6 green onions (scallions), sliced thinly

1 Boil, steam or microwave rice until tender.

2 Meanwhile, place lamb in a medium bowl with five-spice and sesame oil; toss lamb to coat in mixture.

3 Heat half the peanut oil in a wok over high heat; stir-fry lamb, in batches, until browned lightly. Remove from wok.

4 Heat remaining peanut oil in wok; stir-fry garlic, ginger and brown onion for 3 minutes or until onion just softens. Add capsicums and choy sum to wok; stir-fry for 2 minutes or until capsicum is just tender.

5 Blend cornflour with stock and sauces in a small jug. Return lamb to wok, add cornflour mixture; stir-fry until sauce boils and thickens slightly and lamb is heated through and cooked as desired. Serve stir-fry sprinkled with green onion, accompany with rice.

HOISIN SWEET CHILLI LAMB AND VEGETABLE STIR-FRY

PREP + COOK TIME 15 MINUTES ◆ SERVES 4

100g (3 ounces) dried rice vermicelli noodles

1 tablespoon peanut oil

750g (1½ pounds) lamb strips

400g (12½ ounces) fresh mixed vegetables

1 tablespoon finely grated fresh ginger

1 clove garlic, crushed

⅓ cup (80ml) hoisin sauce

2 tablespoons sweet chilli sauce

2 tablespoons water

¼ cup fresh coriander (cilantro) leaves

1 Place noodles in a medium heatproof bowl, cover with boiling water; stand 5 minutes or until noodles are tender, drain.

2 Heat oil in a wok; stir-fry lamb, in batches, for 3 minutes or until cooked through. Remove lamb from wok.

3 Stir-fry vegetables, ginger and garlic in wok for 5 minutes or until almost tender. Return lamb to wok with noodles, sauces and the water; stir-fry until hot. Season to taste; serve sprinkled with coriander.

TEST KITCHEN NOTES

USE YOUR FAVOURITE NOODLES OR RICE INSTEAD OF RICE VERMICELLI NOODLES. BEEF, CHICKEN OR PORK CAN BE SUBSTITUTED FOR LAMB. FOR THE MIXED VEGETABLES, WE USED 1 CAPSICUM, 1 BUNCH PAK CHOY, 1 PACKET OYSTER MUSHROOMS AND 150G (4½ OUNCES) SNOW PEAS. RECIPE IS BEST MADE JUST BEFORE SERVING.

PESTO LAMB WITH ZUCCHINI AND ALMOND SALAD

PREP + COOK TIME 25 MINUTES ◆ SERVES 4

⅓ cup (90g) pesto

4 lamb rump steaks (600g)

ZUCCHINI AND ALMOND SALAD

3 medium zucchini (360g), cut into thin ribbons

⅓ cup (45g) blanched almonds, halved, roasted

1 small fresh red thai (serrano) chilli, chopped finely

1 tablespoon lemon juice

2 tablespoons extra virgin olive oil

1 Combine pesto and lamb in a large bowl. Cook lamb on a heated oiled grill plate (or grill or barbecue), for 4 minutes each side or until cooked as desired. Cover with foil; stand 5 minutes.

2 To make zucchini and almond salad, place zucchini, almonds and chilli in a large bowl; toss with combined juice and oil until zucchini is well coated. Season to taste.

3 Serve lamb with salad.

TEST KITCHEN NOTES

LAMB CAN BE MARINATED IN PESTO 2 HOURS AHEAD OR OVERNIGHT. YOU CAN ALSO USE LAMB CUTLETS. REMOVE MEMBRANES AND SEEDS FROM CHILLI TO LESSEN THE HEAT. DRESS SALAD JUST BEFORE SERVING.

CAJUN LAMB BACKSTRAPS WITH FOUR-BEAN SALAD

PREP + COOK TIME 25 MINUTES ◆ SERVES 4

1 tablespoon cajun seasoning

800g (1½ pounds) lamb backstraps

1 small red onion (100g), chopped finely

400g (12½ ounces) heirloom cherry tomatoes, halved

60g (2 ounces) baby spinach leaves, shredded finely

600g (1¼ pounds) canned four-bean mix, rinsed, drained

¼ cup firmly packed fresh coriander (cilantro) leaves

¼ cup firmly packed fresh flat-leaf parsley

⅓ cup (80ml) bottled french dressing

lemon wedges, to serve

1 Rub seasoning onto lamb; cook lamb on a heated oiled grill plate (or grill or barbecue) for 4 minutes each side or until browned and cooked as desired. Cover; stand 5 minutes, then slice lamb thickly.

2 Meanwhile, place onion, tomatoes, spinach, beans, herbs and dressing in a large bowl; toss gently to combine.

3 Serve salad topped with lamb; accompany with lemon wedges.

TEST KITCHEN NOTES

YOU CAN SUBSTITUTE LAMB RUMP OR LOIN CHOPS FOR BACKSTRAPS.

PORK AND VEGETABLE PANCAKES

PREP + COOK TIME 25 MINUTES ◆ MAKES 12

12 peking duck pancakes (230g)

1 tablespoon peanut oil

250g (8 ounces) minced (ground) pork

100g (3 ounces) fresh shiitake mushrooms, sliced thinly

1 tablespoon chinese cooking wine (shao hsing)

1 tablespoon japanese soy sauce

1 tablespoon oyster sauce

1 teaspoon sesame oil

1 small carrot (70g), cut into matchsticks

2 small lebanese cucumbers (or 250g qukes), cut into lengths

4 green onions (scallions), sliced thinly

1 To heat pancakes, fold each into quarters then place in a steamer over a large pan of simmering water until warm and pliable.

2 Meanwhile, heat peanut oil in a wok over high heat; stir-fry pork for 4 minutes or until browned. Add mushrooms; stir-fry for 4 minutes or until tender.

3 Add wine, sauces and sesame oil to wok; stir-fry until combined. Season to taste.

4 Serve pork mixture with pancakes, carrot, cucumber and onion.

TEST KITCHEN NOTES

PEKING DUCK PANCAKES ARE SMALL PANCAKES MADE WITH PLAIN FLOUR; THEY ARE AVAILABLE FROM ASIAN FOOD STORES AND SUPERMARKETS.

SPICY BEEF NOODLES

PREP + COOK TIME 30 MINUTES ◆ SERVES 4

500g (1 pound) udon noodles

2 tablespoons peanut oil

750g (1½ pounds) minced (ground) beef

1 small brown onion (80g), sliced thinly

2 cloves garlic, crushed

⅓ cup (95g) black bean sauce

2 medium carrots (240g), cut into matchsticks

1 bunch baby pak choy (400g), chopped coarsely

¼ cup (60ml) hoisin sauce

¼ cup (60ml) beef stock

2 tablespoons rice vinegar

2 tablespoons coarsely chopped fresh coriander (cilantro) leaves

1 Place noodles in a large heatproof bowl, cover with hot water; stand 5 minutes, drain.

2 Heat oil in a wok over high heat; stir-fry beef, onion and garlic for 5 minutes or until beef is browned and almost cooked. Add black bean sauce; stir-fry until mixture is well browned.

3 Add noodles, carrot, pak choy, hoisin sauce, stock and vinegar; stir-fry for 3 minutes or until vegetables are just tender. Serve sprinkled with coriander.

TEST KITCHEN NOTES

SWAP BEEF MINCE FOR PORK AND VEAL OR CHICKEN MINCE. USE A VEGETABLE PEELER TO CUT CARROTS. THIS RECIPE IS NOT SUITABLE TO FREEZE.

CHINESE BARBECUED PORK STIR-FRY

PREP + COOK TIME 25 MINUTES ◆ SERVES 4

375g (12 ounces) dried rice stick noodles

1 tablespoon sesame oil

1 clove garlic, crushed

1 fresh small red thai (serrano) chilli, seeded, sliced thinly

250g (8 ounces) mixed mushrooms, sliced thickly

175g (5½ ounces) broccolini, chopped coarsely

2 teaspoons cornflour (cornstarch)

¼ cup (60ml) soy sauce

600g (1¼ pounds) chinese barbecued pork, sliced thickly

1 tablespoon fish sauce

¾ cup (180ml) chicken stock

4 green onions (scallions), sliced thinly

1 Place noodles in a large heatproof bowl, cover with boiling water; stand until just tender, drain.

2 Meanwhile, heat oil in a wok; stir-fry garlic, chilli, mushrooms and broccolini for 3 minutes or until mushrooms are just tender.

3 Blend cornflour with the soy sauce in a small jug. Add cornflour mixture to wok with pork, fish sauce and stock; stir-fry until sauce boils and thickens slightly.

4 Add noodles and onion to wok; stir-fry until mixture is heated through. Serve stir-fry sprinkled with sesame seeds, if you like.

TEST KITCHEN NOTES

USE A MIXTURE OF YOUR FAVOURITE MUSHROOMS IN THIS RECIPE.

CHINESE BARBECUED PORK IS AVAILABLE FROM ASIAN BUTCHERS AND BARBECUED MEAT SHOPS.

GRILLED CHICKEN SALAD

PREP + COOK TIME 25 MINUTES (+ REFRIGERATION & STANDING) ♦ SERVES 4

350g (11 ounces) chicken breast fillets

4 kaffir lime leaves, shredded thinly

1 fresh long red chilli, chopped coarsely

1 tablespoon finely grated fresh ginger

1 clove garlic, crushed

⅓ cup (80ml) lime juice

⅓ cup (80ml) peanut oil

1 lime

2 medium carrots (240g), sliced into long, thin strips

2 lebanese cucumbers (260g), cut lengthways into wedges

500g (1 pound) wide fresh rice noodles

350g (11 ounces) gai lan, chopped coarsely

¼ cup firmly packed fresh coriander (cilantro) leaves

LIME DRESSING

¼ cup (60ml) lime juice

¼ cup (70g) sweet chilli sauce

1 teaspoon soy sauce

1 tablespoon caster (superfine) sugar

2 tablespoons peanut oil

2 tablespoons water

2 kaffir lime leaves, sliced thinly

1 Combine chicken, lime leaves, chilli, ginger, garlic, juice and oil in a large bowl, cover; refrigerate 3 hours or overnight.

2 Cut lime in half, cut each half into three wedges.

3 Drain chicken; discard marinade. Cook chicken on a heated oiled grill plate (or grill or barbecue) for 10 minutes or until browned and cooked through. Cool 5 minutes. Add lime to grill plate; cook about 2 minutes, turning until browned all over. Cover chicken and lime; refrigerate until cold.

4 Place carrot and cucumber into a bowl of iced water; stand 30 minutes, drain.

5 Meanwhile, place noodles in a large heatproof bowl, cover with boiling water; separate with a fork, drain.

6 Boil, steam or microwave gai lan until just tender; drain, cool.

7 To make lime dressing, combine ingredients in a screw-top jar; shake well.

8 Just before serving, slice chicken; place in a large bowl with lime wedges, drained carrot and cucumber, noodles, gai lan, coriander and dressing. Toss gently to combine.

TEST KITCHEN NOTES

THIS RECIPE CAN BE MADE A DAY AHEAD. COVER CHICKEN MIXTURE, VEGETABLES AND DRESSING SEPARATELY AND REFRIGERATE. USE A JULIENNE PEELER TO SLICE CARROT INTO LONG THIN STRIPS.

CHICKEN AND SNAKE BEAN STIR-FRY

PREP + COOK TIME 20 MINUTES ◆ SERVES 4

⅔ cup (130g) jasmine rice

1 tablespoon peanut oil

800g (1½ pounds) chicken thigh fillets, sliced thickly

2 medium white onions (300g), sliced thickly

3 cloves garlic, crushed

1 teaspoon chinese five-spice powder

400g (12½ ounces) snake beans, cut into 5cm (2-inch) lengths

½ cup (125ml) oyster sauce

2 tablespoons light soy sauce

½ cup (75g) cashews, toasted

½ cup loosely packed fresh thai basil leaves

1 fresh long red chilli, sliced thinly diagonally

1 Cook rice according to packet directions until tender; drain.

2 Heat half the oil in a wok over high heat; stir-fry chicken, in batches, until browned all over and cooked through. Remove from wok.

3 Heat remaining oil in wok; stir-fry onion, garlic and five-spice for 3 minutes or until onion softens. Add beans; stir-fry for 4 minutes or until tender.

4 Return chicken to wok with sauces and cashews; stir-fry until sauce boils and thickens slightly.

5 Just before serving, stir in basil. Serve stir-fry with rice; sprinkle with chilli.

TEST KITCHEN NOTES

SNAKE BEANS ARE LONG, THIN GREEN BEANS THAT ARE ASIAN IN ORIGIN; IF UNAVAILABLE, YOU CAN USE GREEN BEANS. IN THIS DISH WE'VE USED THAI BASIL, ALSO KNOWN AS BAI KAPROW OR HOLY BASIL. IF YOU CAN'T FIND IT, USE ORDINARY SWEET BASIL INSTEAD.

SERVING SUGGESTION
REPLACE THE RICE WITH RICE NOODLES, IF YOU PREFER.

SERVING SUGGESTION
STEAMED JASMINE RICE OR SOFTENED RICE STICK NOODLES.

HONEY SOY CHICKEN

PREP + COOK TIME 25 MINUTES (+ REFRIGERATION) ◆ SERVES 4

¼ cup (90g) honey

¼ cup (60ml) soy sauce

½ teaspoon chinese five-spice powder

1 tablespoon dry sherry

1 clove garlic, crushed

1 teaspoon finely grated fresh ginger

700g (1½ pounds) chicken breast fillets, sliced thinly

1 tablespoon peanut oil

1 large brown onion (200g), sliced thinly

1 tablespoon sesame seeds

500g (1 pound) baby pak choy, quartered

500g (1 pound) choy sum, chopped coarsely

2 tablespoons dry roasted peanuts, chopped coarsely

1 fresh long red chilli, sliced thinly

1 Combine honey, sauce, five-spice, sherry, garlic and ginger in a small screw-top jar; shake well. Place chicken in a medium bowl, combine with half the honey mixture; cover, refrigerate 3 hours or overnight. Reserve remaining honey mixture, covered, in the fridge.

2 Drain chicken, discard marinade. Heat half the oil in a wok; stir-fry chicken and onion, in batches, until chicken is browned. Remove from wok.

3 Heat remaining oil in wok; stir-fry seeds until browned lightly. Return chicken to wok with pak choy, choy sum and reserved honey mixture; stir-fry until vegetables are just wilted. Sprinkle with peanuts and chilli to serve.

TEST KITCHEN NOTES

BABY PAK CHOY IS DISTINGUISHED FROM BABY BUK CHOY BY ITS PALE GREEN-COLOURED STEMS, WHILE THE STEMS OF BABY BUK CHOY ARE WHITE.

FISH WITH MIXED VEGETABLES

PREP + COOK TIME 25 MINUTES ◆ SERVES 4

⅔ cup (130g) jasmine rice

500g (1 pound) firm white fish fillets, cut into 3cm (1¼-inch) pieces

2 cloves garlic, chopped finely

2½ tablespoons peanut oil

350g (11 ounces) choy sum, chopped coarsely

1 large carrot (180g), cut into matchsticks

150g (4½ ounces) baby corn, halved lengthways

¼ cup (60ml) oyster sauce

1 tablespoon japanese soy sauce

1 tablespoon water

¼ cup fresh coriander (cilantro) leaves

1 Cook rice according to directions on packet until tender.

2 Meanwhile, combine fish, garlic and 2 tablespoons of the oil in a medium bowl.

3 Heat wok; stir-fry fish mixture, in batches, until browned. Remove from wok.

4 Heat remaining oil in wok; stir-fry choy sum, carrot and corn until tender. Return fish to wok with sauces and the water; stir-fry until hot, season to taste.

5 Sprinkle coriander over stir-fry. Serve with rice and accompany with lemon, if you like.

TEST KITCHEN NOTES

WE USED BLUE-EYE (TREVALLY) FILLETS IN THIS RECIPE, BUT USE ANY FIRM WHITE FISH FILLETS.

ASPARAGUS AND SALMON PASTA

PREP + COOK TIME 25 MINUTES ◆ SERVES 4

375g (12 ounces) spiral pasta

340g (11 ounces) asparagus, trimmed, cut into 5cm (2-inch) lengths

415g (13 ounces) canned red salmon, drained, flaked

100g (3 ounces) watercress, trimmed

3 spring onions (75g), sliced thinly

WHOLEGRAIN MUSTARD VINAIGRETTE

1 clove garlic, crushed

2 tablespoons wholegrain mustard

2 tablespoons red wine vinegar

2 tablespoons lemon juice

¼ cup (60ml) olive oil

1 Cook pasta in a large saucepan of boiling water until just tender; drain. Rinse under cold water; drain.
2 Meanwhile, boil, steam or microwave asparagus until just tender; drain. Rinse under cold water; drain.
3 To make wholegrain mustard vinaigrette, combine ingredients in a screw-top jar; shake well.
4 Combine pasta and asparagus in a large bowl with salmon, watercress and onion. Drizzle dressing over pasta; toss gently to combine.

TEST KITCHEN NOTES

USE YOUR FAVOURITE PASTA OR TRY PENNE, CONCHIGLIE (A SHELL-SHAPED PASTA) OR OTHER SHORT PASTA.

VEGETABLE, HALOUMI AND ROCKET SALAD

PREP + COOK TIME 30 MINUTES ◆ SERVES 4

250g (8 ounces) haloumi cheese, cut into 1cm (½-inch) slices

175g (5½ ounces) vine sweet mini capsicums, halved

3 baby eggplants (180g), chopped coarsely

2 medium zucchini (320g), sliced thickly

½ cup fresh mint leaves

2 tablespoons lemon juice

⅓ cup (95g) Greek-style yoghurt

150g (4½ ounces) baby rocket leaves (arugula)

1   Cook haloumi, capsicum, eggplant and zucchini, in batches, on a heated oiled grill plate (or grill or barbecue) until browned lightly and just tender.

2   Meanwhile, process mint, juice and yoghurt until smooth. Season to taste.

3   Combine haloumi and vegetables in a large bowl with rocket; toss gently to combine. Serve drizzled with dressing.

TEST KITCHEN NOTES

HALOUMI IS A SHEEP-MILK CHEESE THAT CAN BE GRILLED OR FRIED, BRIEFLY, WITHOUT BREAKING DOWN. IT SHOULD BE EATEN WHILE STILL WARM AS IT BECOMES TOUGH AND RUBBERY ON COOLING. IF YOU LIKE, YOU CAN COOK 180G (6 OUNCES) HALVED MUSHROOMS WITH THE HALOUMI AND VEGETABLES. USING A VARIETY OF MUSHROOMS, SUCH AS PORTOBELLO, BUTTON AND SWISS BROWNS, WILL ADD EXTRA FLAVOUR TO THE DISH.

SERVING SUGGESTION TOASTED WHOLEGRAIN SOURDOUGH BREAD.

SERVING
SUGGESTION
GREEN SALAD AND
A LOAF OF FRESH
CRUSTY BREAD.

GNOCCHI WITH HERB AND MUSHROOM SAUCE

PREP + COOK TIME 25 MINUTES ◆ SERVES 4

1 tablespoon vegetable oil

1 medium brown onion (150g), chopped coarsely

2 cloves garlic, crushed

400g (12½ ounces) swiss brown mushrooms, sliced thinly

1 tablespoon plain (all-purpose) flour

⅓ cup (80ml) dry red wine

1 cup (250ml) vegetable stock

1 tablespoon light sour cream

600g (1¼ pounds) fresh potato gnocchi

¼ cup grated parmesan

2 tablespoons micro herbs, optional

1 Heat oil in a large frying pan over medium heat; cook onion, garlic and mushrooms, stirring, for 5 minutes or until vegetables are just tender. Add flour; cook, stirring, about 1 minute.

2 Add wine, stock and sour cream; cook, stirring, until sauce thickens slightly.

3 Meanwhile, cook gnocchi in a large saucepan of boiling water until gnocchi rise to the surface and are just tender; drain. Add gnocchi to mushroom sauce; toss gently to combine. Sprinkle with parmesan and micro herbs to serve.

TEST KITCHEN NOTES

YOU COULD SUBSTITUTE BUTTON OR OYSTER MUSHROOMS FOR THE SWISS BROWNS. WE USED A SHIRAZ-STYLE WINE. GNOCCHI ARE SMALL DUMPLINGS MADE FROM INGREDIENTS SUCH AS FLOUR, POTATOES, SEMOLINA, RICOTTA OR SPINACH.

BROAD BEAN AND RICOTTA ORECCHIETTE

PREP + COOK TIME 30 MINUTES ◆ SERVES 4

375g (12 ounces) orecchiette pasta

½ cup (125ml) extra virgin olive oil

1 clove garlic, bruised

100g (3 ounces) sourdough bread, torn

2 cups (300g) fresh shelled broad beans (fava beans)

1 clove garlic, extra, crushed

1 teaspoon finely grated lemon rind

¼ cup (60ml) lemon juice

200g (6½ ounces) ricotta, crumbled

½ cup fresh mint leaves

1 Cook pasta in a large saucepan of boiling water until almost tender; drain.

2 Meanwhile, heat 2 tablespoons of the oil in a large frying pan over medium heat. Add garlic and bread; stir for 8 minutes or until bread is golden. Transfer bread to a bowl; discard garlic.

3 Heat 1 tablespoon of the oil in same frying pan over medium heat; cook beans and extra garlic for 5 minutes or until beans are just tender. Add pasta, rind, juice and remaining oil; stir until pasta is warmed through.

4 Serve pasta topped with pieces of toasted garlic bread, ricotta and mint.

TEST KITCHEN NOTES

IF FRESH BROAD BEANS AREN'T AVAILABLE USE FROZEN OR SUBSTITUTE WITH PEAS. BASIL CAN BE SUBSTITUTED FOR MINT. SPRINKLE PASTA WITH DRIED CHILLI FLAKES FOR SOME HEAT.

CAULIFLOWER, POTATO AND BEAN CURRY

PREP + COOK TIME 30 MINUTES ◆ SERVES 4

4 eggs

1 medium brown onion (150g), sliced thickly

2 fresh small red thai (serrano) chillies, chopped coarsely

1 clove garlic, crushed

2 tablespoons mild curry paste

500g (1 pound) cauliflower florets

4 small potatoes (480g), chopped coarsely

2 cups (500ml) vegetable stock

2 cups (400g) jasmine rice

200g (6½ ounces) green beans, halved

400ml (12½ ounces) light coconut milk

¼ cup loosely packed fresh coriander (cilantro) leaves

1 Boil eggs in a large saucepan of water for 6 minutes or until hard; cool, then peel and halve.

2 Cook onion, chilli and garlic in a heated oiled large saucepan over medium heat, stirring, for 4 minutes or until onion softens. Stir in paste until fragrant. Add vegetables; cook, stirring, until coated in curry mixture. Add stock, bring to the boil; reduce heat, simmer, covered, for 10 minutes or until potato is just tender.

3 Meanwhile, cook rice according to packet directions until just tender. Cover to keep warm.

4 Stir beans into curry mixture; cook, uncovered, for 3 minutes or until just tender. Stir in coconut milk and egg; simmer, uncovered, until heated through. Serve curry with rice; sprinkle with coriander.

TEST KITCHEN NOTES

ACCOMPANY CURRY WITH PAPPADUMS AND RAITA MADE WITH YOGHURT AND CUCUMBER.

CHICKEN AND SUGAR SNAP PEA PASTA

PREP + COOK TIME 25 MINUTES ◆ SERVES 4

375g (12 ounces) long frill-edged pasta

40g (1½ ounces) butter

1 bunch spring onions (400g), sliced thinly

1 clove garlic, crushed

300g (9½ ounces) sugar snap peas, trimmed

2½ cups (425g) shredded cooked chicken

300ml pouring cream

2 teaspoons wholegrain mustard

2 teaspoons finely grated lemon rind

2 tablespoons lemon juice

50g (1½ ounces) baby spinach

50g (1½ ounces) dry roasted almonds, chopped coarsely

1 Cook pasta in a large saucepan of boiling water until just tender; drain.

2 Meanwhile, melt butter in a medium saucepan over medium heat; cook onion and garlic, stirring, for 4 minutes or until onion is soft. Stir in sugar snap peas and chicken.

3 Stir cream, mustard, rind and juice into pan; cook, stirring, without boiling, for 5 minutes or until thickened.

4 Toss pasta and spinach through sauce; sprinkle with almonds, season to taste.

TEST KITCHEN NOTES

WE USED TRIPOLINE LUNGHE, A LONG RIBBON-SHAPED PASTA WITH FRILLED EDGES. ANY RIBBON PASTA, SUCH AS FETTUCCINE OR PAPPARDELLE, CAN BE USED.

ROCKET AND TOMATO LAMB BURRITO

PREP + COOK TIME 30 MINUTES ◆ SERVES 4

500g (1 pound) minced (ground) lamb

35g (1-ounce) packet taco seasoning mix

400g (12½ ounces) canned crushed tomatoes

425g (13 ounces) canned Mexe beans

¼ cup water

½ small white onion (80g), finely chopped

150g (4½ ounces) yellow cherry tomatoes, quartered

1 clove crushed garlic

1 fresh green chilli, chopped finely

⅓ cup coarsely chopped fresh coriander (cilantro)

4 x 20cm (8-inch) flour tortillas, warmed

50g (1½ ounces) baby rocket leaves (arugula)

¾ cup (90g) grated tasty cheese

1 Cook lamb in a heated oiled pan; stirring for 5 minutes or until browned. Add seasoning mix, tomatoes, beans and the water to pan; boil then reduce heat to medium-low. Simmer, uncovered, for 10 minutes or until mixture thickens; season.

2 Combine onion, tomatoes, garlic, chilli and coriander in a small bowl.

3 Divide lamb mixture between tortillas; top with rocket, tomato mixture and cheese. Season to taste. Fold tortilla to enclose filling.

CREAMY MUSHROOM PASTA

PREP + COOK TIME 25 MINUTES ◆ SERVES 4

375g (12 ounces) penne pasta

300g (9½ ounces) button mushrooms, sliced thinly

300ml pouring cream

½ cup finely grated parmesan

⅓ cup coarsely chopped fresh chives

1 Cook pasta in a large saucepan of boiling water until tender; drain.

2 Cook mushrooms in a heated oiled large frying pan, stirring, for 4 minutes or until soft. Add cream, parmesan and chives; stir over low heat until parmesan melts.

3 Add pasta to mushroom mixture; stir until heated through. Accompany with garlic bread, if you like.

SATAY CHICKEN SKEWERS

PREP + COOK TIME 20 MINUTES ◆ SERVES 4

12 chicken tenderloins (900g)

1 teaspoon curry powder

½ teaspoon each onion powder and garlic powder

¼ teaspoon each ground cumin and ground chilli

2 tablespoons peanut oil

1 large brown onion (200g), grated

2 teaspoons crushed ginger

1 cup (250ml) coconut cream

¾ cup (210g) crunchy peanut butter

2 tablespoons sweet chilli sauce

2 tablespoons light soy sauce

¼ cup (35g) crushed roasted peanuts

450g (14½ ounces) packaged white microwave rice

1 telegraph cucumber (400g), sliced into thin ribbons

1 Heat an oiled chargrill plate (or grill pan or barbecue).

2 Combine chicken, spices and half the oil in a large bowl; season. Thread chicken onto 12 skewers; cook for 3 minutes each side or until cooked through.

3 Meanwhile, heat remaining oil in a small saucepan; cook onion and ginger, stirring, for 1 minute or until onion softens. Add coconut cream, peanut butter, sauces and peanuts; simmer, stirring, about 1 minute.

4 Microwave rice according to packet directions.

5 Serve skewers with rice, peanut sauce and cucumber. Top with fresh coriander and lime wedges, if you like.

TEST KITCHEN NOTES

IF YOU USE BAMBOO SKEWERS, SOAK THEM IN A SHALLOW DISH OF BOILING WATER, THEN DRAIN IMMEDIATELY. THIS WILL PREVENT THEM FROM BURNING DURING COOKING. USE A FOOD PROCESSOR TO GRATE ONION, A VEGETABLE PEELER TO SLICE CUCUMBER AND PREPARED CRUSHED GINGER AVAILABLE IN TUBES FROM SUPERMARKETS.

1

SPICY MEXICAN

PREP + COOK TIME 30 MINUTES ♦ SERVES 4

Mix 500g (1 pound) minced beef in a bowl with 1 small finely chopped onion, 2 tablespoons finely chopped fresh flat-leaf parsley and 1 clove crushed garlic. Shape into 4 patties; cover, refrigerate 15 minutes or until firm. Cook patties in a large frying pan over medium heat for 5 minutes each side or until cooked through. Halve and toast 4 bread rolls. Sandwich rolls with a pattie, 3 thin slices avocado, 3 slices jalapeño chilli and 2 tablespoons grated tasty cheese. Drizzle with mild tomato salsa.

2

ANTIPASTO ITALIAN

PREP + COOK TIME 30 MINUTES ♦ SERVES 4

Mix 500g (1 pound) minced beef in a bowl with 1 small finely chopped onion, 2 tablespoons finely chopped fresh flat-leaf parsley and 1 clove crushed garlic. Shape into 4 patties; cover, refrigerate 15 minutes or until firm. Cook patties in a large frying pan over medium heat for 5 minutes each side or until cooked through. Halve and toast 4 bread rolls. Spread bases with sun-dried tomato pesto. Sandwich rolls with a pattie, 1 slice char-grilled eggplant and a quarter of a char-grilled capsicum. Evenly divide 1 tablespoon each shaved parmesan and fresh basil leaves between rolls.

BURGERS

3

BACON AND EGG

PREP + COOK TIME 30 MINUTES ♦ SERVES 4

Mix 500g (1 pound) minced beef in a bowl with 1 small finely chopped onion, 2 tablespoons finely chopped fresh flat-leaf parsley and 1 clove crushed garlic. Shape into 4 patties; cover, refrigerate 15 minutes or until firm. Cook patties in a large frying pan over medium heat for 5 minutes each side or until cooked through. Remove patties from pan; cover to keep warm. In the same frying pan cook 4 rindless bacon slices until crisp, drain on paper towel. Fry 4 eggs in pan until cooked to your liking. Halve and toast 4 bread rolls. Spread bases with barbecue sauce. Sandwich rolls with a pattie, 1 slice bacon and an egg.

4

CLASSIC BEEF

PREP + COOK TIME 30 MINUTES ♦ SERVES 4

Mix 500g (1 pound) minced beef in a bowl with 1 small finely chopped onion, 2 tablespoons finely chopped fresh flat-leaf parsley and 1 clove crushed garlic. Shape into 4 patties; cover, refrigerate 15 minutes or until firm. Cook patties in a large frying pan over medium heat for 5 minutes each side or until cooked through. Halve and toast 4 bread rolls. Sandwich rolls with a lettuce leaf, a pattie, a drizzle of tomato sauce, a slice of tasty cheese and a slice of tomato.

1

STEAMED GAI LAN IN OYSTER SAUCE

PREP + COOK TIME 10 MINUTES ◆ SERVES 8

Boil, steam or microwave 1kg (2 pounds) halved gai lan until tender; drain. Heat 1 tablespoon peanut oil in a wok; stir-fry gai lan, 2 tablespoons oyster sauce and 1 tablespoon light soy sauce for 2 minutes or until mixture is heated through.

2

BRUSSELS SPROUTS WITH CREAM AND ALMONDS

PREP + COOK TIME 10 MINUTES ◆ SERVES 4

Melt 10g (½ ounce) butter in a large frying pan; cook ⅓ cup flaked almonds, stirring, until browned lightly; remove from pan. Melt 40g (1½ ounces) extra butter in same pan; cook 1kg (2 pounds) halved brussels sprouts and 2 crushed garlic cloves, stirring, until sprouts are browned lightly. Add 300ml pouring cream; bring to the boil. Reduce heat; simmer, uncovered, until sprouts are tender and sauce thickens slightly. Serve sprout mixture sprinkled with nuts.

SIDES

3

MIXED BEAN SALAD WITH HAZELNUT BUTTER

PREP + COOK TIME 15 MINUTES ◆ SERVES 4

Boil, steam or microwave 250g (8 ounces) each trimmed green beans and yellow beans until tender; drain. Combine warm beans with 60g (2 ounces) chopped butter, ⅓ cup finely chopped roasted hazelnuts, ½ cup torn flat-leaf parsley and 2 teaspoons finely grated lemon rind in a medium bowl.

4

PEAS WITH MINT BUTTER

PREP + COOK TIME 10 MINUTES ◆ SERVES 4

Boil, steam or microwave 2¼ cups fresh shelled peas until tender; drain. Meanwhile, combine 40g (1½ ounces) butter, 1 tablespoon finely chopped fresh mint and 1 tablespoon thinly sliced lemon rind in a small bowl. Serve peas topped with butter mixture.

TIP
You will need approximately 1kg (2 pounds) fresh pea pods to get the amount of shelled peas needed for this recipe.

LIGHT

EATING LIGHTLY ISN'T
ABOUT CUTTING BACK —
IT'S ABOUT EATING FRESH,
SUMMERY FOOD. CREATE
MEALS AROUND DELICIOUS
SEASONAL PRODUCE USED
AT ITS PEAK AND YOUR
FAMILY WILL FEEL LIGHTER.

SERVING
SUGGESTION
STEAMED RICE OR
RICE NOODLES.

FIVE-SPICE BEEF WITH ALMONDS

PREP + COOK TIME 35 MINUTES ◆ SERVES 4

750g (1½-pound) piece beef eye-fillet, sliced thinly

1 teaspoon garam masala

2 teaspoons chinese five-spice powder

1 tablespoon peanut oil

1 medium carrot (120g), cut into long thin strips

1 large red capsicum (bell pepper) (350g), cut into long thin strips

2 cloves garlic, crushed

1 tablespoon finely grated fresh ginger

170g (5½ ounces) coarsely chopped choy sum

3 teaspoons sambal oelek

2 tablespoons oyster sauce

2 tablespoons mango chutney

2 tablespoons lime juice

2 tablespoons water

100g (3 ounces) snow peas, trimmed

1 cup (80g) bean sprouts

⅓ cup (55g) blanched almonds, toasted, chopped roughly

1 Combine beef and spices in a large bowl; mix well.

2 Heat half the oil in a wok over high heat; stir-fry beef mixture, in batches, until beef is browned and tender, remove from wok.

3 Heat remaining oil in wok; add carrot, capsicum, garlic and ginger. Stir-fry about 2 minutes, then add choy sum, sambal, sauce, chutney, juice and the water; stir-fry for 4 minutes or until choy sum is tender.

4 Return beef to wok with snow peas and sprouts; stir-fry until heated through. Serve topped with almonds.

TEST KITCHEN NOTES

YOU CAN SUBSTITUTE BEEF WITH CHICKEN OR PORK. THIS RECIPE IS NOT SUITABLE TO FREEZE.

THAI BEEF OMELETTES

PREP + COOK TIME 30 MINUTES ◆ SERVES 4

2 tablespoons peanut oil

400g (14½ ounces) beef rump steak, sliced thinly

1 small brown onion (80g), sliced thinly

2 cloves garlic, crushed

2 tablespoons oyster sauce

8 eggs

1 teaspoon fish sauce

1 teaspoon soy sauce

100g (3 ounces) enoki mushrooms

½ cup each fresh mint and thai basil leaves

1 cup (80g) bean sprouts

1 long red chilli, seeded, cut into strips

1 Heat 2 teaspoons of the oil in a wok over high heat; stir-fry beef, in batches, until browned. Remove from wok.

2 Heat another 2 teaspoons of the oil in wok; stir-fry onion and garlic until fragrant. Return beef to wok with oyster sauce; stir-fry until hot. Remove from wok; cover to keep warm.

3 Whisk eggs with fish and soy sauces in a large jug. Heat 1 teaspoon of the oil in same wok; pour in a ¼ cup of the egg mixture, tilting the wok to make a 14cm (5½-inch) omelette, cook until almost set. Slide omelette onto a serving plate; cover to keep warm. Repeat to make a total of eight omelettes.

4 Fill omelettes with beef, mushrooms, herbs, sprouts and chilli.

TEST KITCHEN NOTES

TO MAKE A 'NET-STYLE' OMELETTE, PLACE EGG MIXTURE IN A PLASTIC ZIPTOP BAG. SNIP A SMALL HOLE IN ONE CORNER AND DRIZZLE THE MIXTURE INTO A HEATED OILED WOK.

ENOKI
MUSHROOMS
HAVE CLUMPS OF LONG,
SPAGHETTI-LIKE STEMS
WITH TINY, SNOWY
WHITE CAPS. THEY ARE
AVAILABLE FROM ASIAN
FOOD SHOPS AND
SUPERMARKETS.

BEEF STEAK WITH CAPSICUM RELISH

PREP + COOK TIME 30 MINUTES ◆ SERVES 4

3 medium red capsicums (bell pepper) (600g)

1 teaspoon olive oil

1 large brown onion (200g), sliced thinly

2 cloves garlic, sliced thinly

2 tablespoons brown sugar

2 tablespoons sherry vinegar

3 fresh small red thai (serrano) chillies, seeded, chopped finely

4 x 200g (6½-ounce) beef eye-fillet steaks

2 corn cobs (800g), trimmed, chopped coarsely

150g (4½ ounces) sugar snap peas

300g (9½ ounces) baby new (chat) potatoes

2 tablespoons coarsely chopped fresh flat-leaf parsley

1 Preheat grill (broiler).

2 Quarter capsicums; discard seeds and membranes. Roast under grill, skin-side up, until skin blisters and blackens. Cover with plastic or paper for 5 minutes, then peel away skin; slice flesh thinly.

3 Heat oil in a medium frying pan over high heat; cook onion and garlic, stirring, for 3 minutes or until soft. Add sugar, vinegar, chilli and capsicum; cook, stirring, about 5 minutes. Season to taste.

4 Cook beef on a heated oiled grill plate (or grill or barbecue) for 4 minutes each side or until browned and cooked as desired. Cover; stand 5 minutes.

5 Meanwhile, boil, steam or microwave corn, peas and potatoes, separately, until just tender; drain.

6 Top steaks with capsicum relish; serve with vegetables, sprinkle with parsley.

TEST KITCHEN NOTES

BEEF RIB-EYE (SCOTCH FILLET) OR SIRLOIN (NEW-YORK CUT) STEAK CAN BE SUBSTITUTED FOR EYE-FILLET. MAKE CAPSICUM RELISH A DAY AHEAD; STORE, COVERED, IN THE REFRIGERATOR. REHEAT JUST BEFORE SERVING.

BEEF AND NOODLE STIR-FRY

PREP + COOK TIME 35 MINUTES ◆ SERVES 4

250g (8 ounces) dried rice stick noodles

2 teaspoons peanut oil

500g (1 pound) beef eye-fillet steaks, sliced thinly

1 tablespoon finely chopped lemon grass, white part only

1 clove garlic, crushed

⅔ cup (160ml) lime juice

⅓ cup (80ml) fish sauce

1 tablespoon coarsely grated palm sugar

100g (3 ounces) chinese mustard leaf, chopped coarsely

1 cup (80g) bean sprouts

½ cup loosely packed fresh coriander (cilantro) leaves

½ cup loosely packed fresh mint leaves

3 green onions (scallions), sliced thinly

1 lebanese cucumber (130g), sliced thinly

1 Place noodles in a large heatproof bowl, cover with boiling water; stand 5 minutes or until tender, drain.

2 Heat half the oil in a wok; stir-fry beef, in batches, until browned. Remove from wok.

3 Heat remaining oil in wok; stir-fry lemon grass and garlic until fragrant. Return beef to wok with juice, sauce and sugar; stir-fry until heated through. Add noodles; stir-fry until combined. Stir in remaining ingredients; serve immediately.

TEST KITCHEN NOTES

USE ANY ASIAN GREENS YOU LIKE INSTEAD OF CHINESE MUSTARD LEAF; TRY BABY TATSOI LEAVES OR CHINESE WATER SPINACH. BABY SPINACH LEAVES COULD ALSO BE USED. RICE STICK NOODLES, ALSO KNOWN AS SEN LEK (THAI) AND HO FUN (CHINESE), ARE WIDE, FLAT NOODLES MADE FROM RICE FLOUR.

SERVING SUGGESTION

SPRINKLE WITH THINLY SLICED RED THAI CHILLI FOR A KICK OF HEAT.

MEXICAN BEEF WRAPS

PREP + COOK TIME 40 MINUTES (+ REFRIGERATION) ◆ SERVES 4

800g (1½ pounds) beef fillet, trimmed, sliced thinly

35g (1-ounce) packet taco seasoning mix

3 cloves garlic, crushed

½ cup (125ml) olive oil

2 large avocados (640g), halved, cut into thin wedges

250g (8 ounces) baby roma tomatoes, quartered

3 green onions (scallions), cut into 5cm (2-inch) lengths, shredded

20 fresh baby coriander (cilantro) sprigs

8 x 20cm (8-inch) flour tortillas, grilled

LIME AND CHILLI MAYONNAISE

1 cup (300g) whole-egg mayonnaise

1½ tablespoons finely grated lime rind

2 tablespoons lime juice

2 tablespoons finely chopped fresh coriander (cilantro)

2 tablespoons finely chopped fresh mint

1½ tablespoons chilli paste

1 Combine beef, seasoning mix, garlic and half the oil in a large bowl. Cover; refrigerate 3 hours or overnight.

2 To make lime and chilli mayonnaise, combine ingredients in a small bowl; season to taste.

3 Heat remaining oil in a large frying pan over high heat. Cook beef, in batches, for 6 minutes or until cooked through. Drain on paper towel.

4 Divide mayonnaise mixture, beef, avocado, tomato, onion and coriander among tortillas. Serve with lemon cheeks, if you like.

TEST KITCHEN NOTES

SUBSTITUTE CHICKEN, LAMB OR PORK FOR THE BEEF, IF PREFERRED.

TANDOORI LAMB CUTLETS WITH TOMATO AND CORIANDER SALSA

PREP + COOK TIME 30 MINUTES ♦ SERVES 4

⅔ cup (130g) basmati rice

¼ cup (75g) tandoori paste

¼ cup (70g) Greek-style yoghurt

1 tablespoon lemon juice

12 french-trimmed lamb cutlets (600g)

TOMATO AND CORIANDER SALSA

200g (6½ ounces) grape tomatoes, halved

1 small red onion (100g), chopped finely

2 tablespoons fresh micro coriander (cilantro)

1 Boil, steam or microwave rice until tender; drain.

2 Combine paste, yoghurt and juice in a large bowl; add lamb, turn to coat in mixture. Season.

3 Cook lamb on a heated oiled grill plate (or grill or barbecue) for 4 minutes each side or until browned and cooked as desired. Cover; stand 5 minutes.

4 To make tomato and coriander salsa, combine ingredients in a small bowl; season to taste.

5 Serve lamb with rice and salsa.

TEST KITCHEN NOTES

TO MAKE CHAR-GRILL MARKS WITH NO STICKING OR MESS, LINE THE GRILL PLATE WITH BAKING PAPER.

SERVING SUGGESTION
ACCOMPANY WITH MINI PAPPADUMS OR NAAN BREAD AND MINT RAITA.

LEMON AND GARLIC KEBABS WITH GREEK SALAD

PREP + COOK TIME 30 MINUTES ◆ SERVES 4

8 x 15cm (6-inch) stalks fresh rosemary

800g (1½ pounds) lamb fillets, cut into 3cm (1¼-inch) pieces

3 cloves garlic, crushed

2 tablespoons olive oil

2 teaspoons finely grated lemon rind

1 tablespoon lemon juice

GREEK SALAD

375g (12 ounces) baby roma (egg) tomatoes, halved, cut into wedges

2 lebanese cucumbers (260g), halved lengthways, sliced thinly

1 medium red capsicum (bell pepper) (200g), chopped coarsely

1 medium red onion (170g), sliced thinly

¼ cup (40g) pitted black olives

200g (6½ ounces) fetta, crumbled coarsely

2 teaspoons small fresh oregano leaves

¼ cup (60ml) extra virgin olive oil

2 tablespoons cider vinegar

1 Remove leaves from the bottom two-thirds of each rosemary stalk; sharpen trimmed ends into a point.

2 Thread lamb onto rosemary skewers. Brush kebabs with combined garlic, oil, rind and juice. Cover; refrigerate until required.

3 To make greek salad, combine ingredients in a large bowl; toss gently.

4 Cook kebabs on a heated oiled grill plate (or grill or barbecue) about 10 minutes, turning and brushing with remaining garlic mixture, until cooked.

5 Serve kebabs with greek salad.

TEST KITCHEN NOTES

USE WOODEN SKEWERS, IF YOU PREFER, BUT ADD 2 TEASPOONS CHOPPED FRESH ROSEMARY TO GARLIC MIXTURE.

LAMB WITH CHERMOULLA AND LEMON COUSCOUS

PREP + COOK TIME 25 MINUTES (+ REFRIGERATION) ◆ SERVES 4

2 tablespoons coarsely grated lemon rind

2 cloves garlic, chopped coarsely

2 small fresh red thai (serrano) chillies, chopped coarsely

1 tablespoon finely grated fresh ginger

¼ cup each coarsely chopped fresh flat-leaf parsley and coriander leaves

1 teaspoon sweet paprika

¼ cup (60ml) olive oil

8 trimmed lamb round steaks (1.2kg)

200g (6½ ounces) fresh green and yellow beans

2 tablespoons coarsely chopped fresh coriander (cilantro) leaves, extra

LEMON COUSCOUS

1 small red onion (100g), sliced thinly

1½ cups (300g) pearl couscous

2 cups (500ml) boiling water

40g (1½ ounces) butter

1 tablespoon grated lemon rind

1 tablespoon lemon juice

⅓ cup (25g) unsalted pistachios, chopped coarsely

1 Blend or process rind, garlic, chilli, ginger, herbs, paprika and oil until just combined. Place lamb in a single layer in a shallow dish; coat lamb in mixture. Cover; refrigerate 3 hours or overnight.

2 Cook lamb, in batches, on a heated oiled grill plate (or grill or barbecue) for 4 minutes each side or until cooked as desired. Cover; stand 5 minutes.

3 To make lemon couscous, cook onion in an oiled frying pan until golden. Add couscous and the boiling water; cover, stand 10 minutes or until liquid is absorbed, stirring occasionally. Stir in butter, rind, juice and pistachios; season to taste.

4 Steam, boil or microwave beans until tender; drain.

5 Serve lamb with lemon couscous and beans; sprinkle with extra coriander.

LEMON AND ROSEMARY PORK CUTLETS

PREP + COOK TIME 35 MINUTES ◆ SERVES 4

2 teaspoons finely grated lemon rind

⅓ cup (80ml) lemon juice

1 tablespoon finely chopped fresh rosemary

2 tablespoons olive oil

4 pork cutlets (940g)

120g (4 ounces) curly endive

⅔ cup (180g) drained char-grilled capsicum (bell pepper)

½ small red onion (50g), sliced thinly

100g (3 ounces) marinated fetta, drained, crumbled

1 Combine rind, juice, rosemary and oil in a small jug, place half the mixture in a medium bowl with pork; turn to coat pork in mixture. Reserve remaining lemon mixture.

2 Cook pork in a heated oiled large frying pan, over medium heat, for 4 minutes each side or until browned and cooked as desired.

3 Combine endive, capsicum, onion and remaining lemon mixture in a large bowl; season to taste. Sprinkle with fetta.

4 Serve pork with salad; sprinkle with extra rosemary leaves, if you like.

TEST KITCHEN NOTES

IN THE COOLER MONTHS, SERVE CUTLETS WITH MASHED POTATO AND STEAMED VEGETABLES.

WARM PESTO CHICKEN WITH TOMATO SALAD

PREP + COOK TIME 30 MINUTES (+ REFRIGERATION) ◆ SERVES 4

500g (1 pound) chicken tenderloins

⅓ cup (90g) sun-dried tomato pesto

¼ cup (40g) pine nuts, toasted

TOMATO SALAD

100g (3 ounces) baby spinach leaves

600g (1¼ pounds) mixed tomatoes, seeded, chopped coarsely

1 medium red onion (170g), sliced thinly

2 tablespoons lemon juice

2 tablespoons extra virgin olive oil

½ teaspoon cracked black pepper

1 Combine chicken and pesto in a large bowl, cover; refrigerate 3 hours or overnight.

2 Preheat oven to 200°C/400°F.

3 Place chicken on a wire rack over a baking dish; roast, uncovered, for 25 minutes or until chicken is cooked. Cover; stand 5 minutes.

4 Meanwhile, to make tomato salad, toss ingredients in a medium bowl; season to taste.

5 Serve chicken with tomato salad; sprinkle with pine nuts.

TAMARIND HONEY PRAWNS WITH PINEAPPLE

PREP + COOK TIME 35 MINUTES ◆ SERVES 4

270g (8½-ounce) packet udon noodles

1.2kg (2½ pounds) uncooked medium king prawns (shrimp)

1 tablespoon vegetable oil

3 cloves garlic, crushed

1 fresh long red chilli, sliced thinly

1 medium red capsicum (bell pepper) (200g), sliced thinly

150g (4½ ounces) snow peas, trimmed

⅓ cup (100g) tamarind concentrate (puree)

2 tablespoons kecap manis

1 tablespoon honey

½ cup (125ml) water

½ small pineapple (450g), chopped coarsely

4 green onions (scallions), sliced thinly

1 tablespoon sesame seeds, toasted

1 Place noodles in a large heatproof bowl, cover with boiling water, separate with a fork; stand 5 minutes or until tender, drain.

2 Meanwhile, shell and devein prawns, leaving tails intact.

3 Heat oil in a wok; stir-fry prawns, garlic, chilli, capsicum and snow peas until prawns are changed in colour. Add remaining ingredients, except sesame seeds; stir-fry until hot.

4 Serve stir-fry with noodles, sprinkle with seeds.

TEST KITCHEN NOTES

SUBSTITUTE RICE OR HOKKIEN NOODLES FOR UDON NOODLES, IF YOU PREFER. TAMARIND ADDS A TART, SWEET/SOUR FLAVOUR TO FOOD. IT IS AVAILABLE FROM ASIAN GROCERS.

CRAB CAKES WITH APPLE SALAD

PREP + COOK TIME 45 MINUTES (+ REFRIGERATION) ◆ SERVES 6

500g (1 pound) fresh cooked white crab meat

½ cup (150g) whole-egg mayonnaise

1 teaspoon finely grated lemon rind

475g (15-ounce) tub mashed potato

1 tablespoon each finely chopped fresh chives and fresh flat-leaf parsley

⅓ cup (35g) plain (all-purpose) flour

2 eggs, beaten lightly

1 cup (75g) panko (japanese) breadcrumbs

60g (2 ounces) ghee

APPLE SALAD

2 tablespoons white wine vinegar

⅓ cup (80ml) olive oil

1 teaspoon dijon mustard

3 medium green-skinned apples (450g), cut into matchsticks

1 bunch red radishes, sliced thinly

1½ cups packed fresh coriander (cilantro) leaves

1 To make apple salad, whisk vinegar, oil and mustard in a medium bowl until combined. Add apple, radish and coriander; toss gently to combine, season to taste.

2 Drain crab meat on paper towel.

3 Stir mayonnaise and rind in a medium bowl; stir in crab, potato and herbs, season. Shape mixture into 12 patties; dust patties in flour, dip in egg, then coat in breadcrumbs. Refrigerate, covered, 30 minutes.

4 Heat ghee in a large frying pan; cook patties, in batches, until browned lightly on both sides, drain.

5 Serve crab cakes with apple salad and lemon wedges, if you like.

PASTA PRIMAVERA WITH POACHED SALMON

PREP + COOK TIME 40 MINUTES ◆ SERVES 4

300g (9½ ounces) fettuccine

1.25 litres (5 cups) water

2 sprigs fresh dill

6 black peppercorns

2 teaspoons finely grated lemon rind

440g (14 ounces) skinless salmon fillets

2 teaspoons olive oil

1 medium red onion (170g), sliced thinly

2 cloves garlic, crushed

170g (5½ ounces) asparagus, halved crossways

150g (4½ ounces) snow peas, halved, trimmed

½ cup (60g) frozen peas

2 tablespoons lemon juice

2 teaspoons finely chopped fresh dill

2 tablespoons coarsely chopped fresh flat-leaf parsley

1 Cook pasta in a large saucepan of boiling water until tender; drain.

2 Meanwhile, place the water, dill sprigs, peppercorns and half the rind in a large saucepan; add salmon. Bring pan to the boil. Reduce heat to medium-low; simmer, uncovered, about 8 minutes, turning salmon halfway through poaching time. Remove salmon from poaching liquid; discard liquid. When salmon is cool enough to handle, flake salmon into a medium bowl.

3 Heat oil in same cleaned pan; cook onion, garlic and asparagus, stirring, until asparagus is tender. Add snow peas, peas, juice, remaining rind, pasta and salmon to pan; stir until hot. Remove from heat; stir in herbs.

TEST KITCHEN NOTES

YOU MAY NEED A LITTLE MORE LIQUID IN THE FINAL PASTA DISH. JUST IN CASE, RESERVE ½ CUP OF THE PASTA COOKING LIQUID AND ADD AS REQUIRED.

HOKKIEN

ARE PLUMP, YELLOW, FRESH WHEAT NOODLES. A POPULAR STIR-FRY NOODLE, THEY ALSO COME IN A THIN VERSION, WHICH CAN BE USED INTERCHANGEABLY WITH SINGAPORE NOODLES.

PRAWN TAMARIND STIR-FRY WITH BUK CHOY

PREP + COOK TIME 35 MINUTES ◆ SERVES 4

450g (14½ ounces) hokkien noodles

750g (1½ pounds) uncooked medium king prawns (shrimp)

2 tablespoons peanut oil

4 green onions (scallions), sliced thinly lengthways

4 cloves garlic, sliced thinly

2 teaspoons cornflour (cornstarch)

1 cup (250ml) vegetable stock

⅓ cup (80ml) oyster sauce

2 tablespoons tamarind concentrate (puree)

2 teaspoons sambal oelek

1 tablespoon sesame oil

2 tablespoons lime juice

2 tablespoons brown sugar

200g (6½ ounces) yellow patty-pan squash, sliced thickly

150g (4½ ounces) sugar snap peas, trimmed

500g (1 pound) baby buk choy, chopped coarsely

1 Cook noodles according to packet directions until tender. Cover to keep warm.

2 Meanwhile, shell and devein prawns leaving tails intact.

3 Heat half the peanut oil in a wok over high heat; stir-fry onion and garlic, separately, until browned lightly. Drain on paper towel.

4 Blend cornflour and stock in a small jug; stir in sauce, tamarind, sambal, sesame oil, juice and sugar.

5 Heat remaining peanut oil in wok; stir-fry prawns, in batches, for 3 minutes or until just changed in colour and almost cooked through. Remove from wok.

6 Add squash to wok; stir-fry for 4 minutes or until just tender. Add cornflour mixture; stir-fry until sauce boils and thickens slightly. Return prawns to wok with peas and buk choy; stir-fry for 2 minutes or until buk choy just wilts and prawns are cooked through.

7 Serve stir-fry with noodles; top with reserved onion and garlic.

TEST KITCHEN NOTES

SHELL PRAWNS WHEN YOU GET HOME AND STORE IN A COVERED BOWL IN THE FRIDGE. PRAWNS ARE BEST USED ON THE DAY OF PURCHASE, ALTHOUGH THEY WILL LAST UP TO 2 DAYS IN THE FRIDGE IF STORED CORRECTLY.

CHINESE BARBECUED DUCK SALAD

PREP + COOK TIME 35 MINUTES ◆ SERVES 4

1 chinese barbecued duck

200g (6½ ounces) dried rice stick noodles

¾ cup each loosely packed fresh coriander (cilantro) and mint leaves

2 lebanese cucumbers (260g), seeded, sliced thinly

½ cup (75g) toasted cashews

CHILLI LIME DRESSING

1 fresh long green chilli, seeded, chopped finely

1 stalk fresh lemon grass, chopped finely

1 clove garlic, crushed

1 teaspoon coarsely grated lime rind

⅓ cup (80ml) lime juice

2 tablespoons peanut oil

1½ tablespoons brown sugar

1½ tablespoons fish sauce

2 teaspoons sesame oil

1 Remove flesh from duck with skin; chop coarsely. Discard bones.

2 Place noodles in a medium heatproof bowl, cover with boiling water; stand 5 minutes or until just tender, drain. Rinse under cold water; drain.

3 To make chilli lime dressing, combine ingredients in a screw-top jar; shake well.

4 Combine duck and noodles in a large bowl with herbs and cucumber; drizzle with dressing, toss gently to combine. Top with cashews before serving.

TEST KITCHEN NOTES

SUBSTITUTE BARBECUED CHICKEN FOR DUCK, IF YOU LIKE. SERVE WITH SLICED RED CHILLI, THINLY SLICED GREEN ONION AND LIME WEDGES.

CHAR-GRILLED CUTTLEFISH, ROCKET AND PARMESAN SALAD

PREP + COOK TIME 30 MINUTES ◆ SERVES 4

1kg (2 pounds) cuttlefish hoods

2 tablespoons olive oil

1 tablespoon finely grated lemon rind

⅓ cup (80ml) lemon juice

1 clove garlic, crushed

150g (4½ ounces) rocket (arugula)

1 small radicchio (150g), leaves separated

200g (6½ ounces) yellow cherry tomatoes, halved

1 small red onion (100g), sliced thinly

1 tablespoon rinsed, drained baby capers

1 cup (80g) shaved parmesan

2 tablespoons balsamic vinegar

⅓ cup (80ml) olive oil, extra

1 Halve cuttlefish lengthways, score insides in a crosshatch pattern, then cut into 5cm (2-inch) strips. Combine cuttlefish in a medium bowl with oil, rind, juice and garlic, cover; refrigerate 10 minutes.

2 Meanwhile, combine rocket, radicchio, tomato, onion, capers and parmesan in a large bowl.

3 Drain cuttlefish; discard marinade. Cook cuttlefish, in batches, on a heated oiled grill plate (or grill or barbecue) for 4 minutes or until browned and cooked through.

4 Add cuttlefish to salad with combined vinegar and extra oil; toss gently to combine.

KIPFLER
POTATOES
ARE GREAT IN SALADS
BECAUSE THEY HOLD
THEIR SHAPE WELL
WHEN COOKED.

HOT-SMOKED SALMON SALAD

PREP + COOK TIME 30 MINUTES ◆ SERVES 4

500g (1 pound) kipfler (fingerling) potatoes

400g (12½ ounces) hot-smoked salmon

100g (3 ounces) snow pea tendrils

1 medium avocado (250g), chopped coarsely

1 lebanese cucumber (130g), halved, sliced thinly

1 small fennel bulb (200g), trimmed, sliced thinly

¼ cup (50g) rinsed, drained baby capers

1 tablespoon dijon mustard

2 teaspoons white (granulated) sugar

2 tablespoons olive oil

1 tablespoon lemon juice

1 Boil, steam or microwave potatoes until just tender; drain. Slice into wedges.

2 Meanwhile, remove any skin and bones from salmon; flake salmon into large pieces. Arrange salmon, potato, tendrils, avocado, cucumber, fennel and capers on a large platter.

3 Combine remaining ingredients in a screw-top jar; shake well, season to taste. Drizzle dressing over salad before serving.

TEST KITCHEN NOTES

BOTH HOT AND COLD-SMOKED SALMON ARE EITHER BRINED OR CURED FIRST. THE DIFFERENCE IS THAT HOT-SMOKED SALMON IS SMOKED AT A HIGHER TEMPERATURE FOR A SHORT PERIOD OF TIME RESULTING IN SALMON THAT CAN BE FLAKED RATHER THAN SLICED. AFTER CURING, COLD-SMOKED SALMON IS SMOKED AT A LOW TEMPERATURE FOR LONGER; THE TEXTURE OF THE FISH IS SIMILAR TO THAT OF RAW FISH IN THAT IT IS EASILY SLICED BUT NOT FLAKED.

FISH FILLETS WITH GRILLED CORN SALAD

PREP + COOK TIME 35 MINUTES ◆ SERVES 4

4 x 200g (6½ ounces) murray cod fillets

2 tablespoons soy sauce

GRILLED CORN SALAD

2 corn cobs (500g), silk and husks removed

250g (8 ounces) cherry tomatoes, halved

1 small red onion (100g), sliced thinly

1 fresh small red thai (serrano) chilli, sliced thinly

2 medium avocados (500g), chopped coarsely

¼ cup coarsely chopped fresh coriander (cilantro)

⅓ cup (80ml) lime juice

1 clove garlic, crushed

1 tablespoon olive oil

1 To make grilled corn salad, cook corn on a heated oiled grill plate (or grill or barbecue) until browned and just tender; cool 10 minutes. Using a sharp knife, remove kernels from cob; combine in a medium bowl with remaining ingredients.

2 Brush fish with sauce; cook on a heated lightly oiled grill plate (or grill or barbecue) for 3 minutes each side or until browned and cooked through.

3 Serve fish with salad.

TEST KITCHEN NOTES

REMOVE FISH FROM PACKAGING BEFORE REFRIGERATING; PLACE THE FILLETS ON A PLATE OR IN A SHALLOW BOWL AND COVER. THIS WILL KEEP FISH FRESHER FOR LONGER.

SERVING SUGGESTION
ACCOMPANY WITH CRUSTY BREAD.

ROASTED CAPSICUM AND LABNE SALAD

PREP + COOK TIME 30 MINUTES ◆ SERVES 4

2 medium orange capsicums (bell pepper) (400g)

2 medium red capsicums (bell pepper) (400g)

2 medium yellow capsicums (bell pepper) (400g)

2 medium green capsicums (bell pepper) (400g)

80g (2½ ounces) baby rocket leaves (arugula)

1 small red onion (100g), sliced thinly

300g (9½ ounces) labne, drained

2 tablespoons fresh oregano leaves

1 teaspoon za'atar

½ teaspoon chilli flakes

RED WINE VINAIGRETTE

⅓ cup (80ml) olive oil

2 tablespoons red wine vinegar

1 clove garlic, crushed

1 Preheat oven to 200°C/400°F.

2 Quarter capsicums; discard seeds and membranes. Place, skin-side up, on an oven tray. Roast, uncovered, for 20 minutes or until skin blisters and blackens. Cover capsicum with plastic or paper 5 minutes; peel away skin, then slice thickly.

3 To make red wine vinaigrette, combine ingredients in a screw-top jar; shake well.

4 Combine capsicum with rocket and onion in a large bowl, add vinaigrette; toss to combine, season. Arrange salad on a large platter, top with labne and oregano; sprinkle with za'atar and chilli.

TEST KITCHEN NOTES

CAPSICUMS CAN ALSO BE GRILLED (BROILED) TO REMOVE THE SKIN.

1

LEMON AND OREGANO

PREP + COOK TIME 30 MINUTES ♦ SERVES 4

Combine 750g (1½ pounds) uncooked prawns, peeled with tails intact, with 2 teaspoons finely grated lemon rind, 2 tablespoons lemon juice, 1 tablespoon extra virgin olive oil and 1 tablespoon chopped fresh oregano in a large bowl. Thread prawns onto 12 bamboo skewers; season. Preheat oiled grill plate (or grill or barbecue); cook skewers until brown all over and prawns are cooked through. Serve skewers with mixed lettuce leaves and flat bread.

2

SUMAC AND LEMON

PREP + COOK TIME 30 MINUTES ♦ SERVES 4

Cut 750g (1½ pounds) firm white fish fillets into 2.5cm (1-inch) pieces. Combine fish with 2 teaspoons sumac, 1 tablespoon lemon juice and 1 tablespoon extra virgin olive oil in a large bowl. Thread fish onto 12 bamboo skewers; season. Preheat oiled grill plate (or grill or barbecue); cook skewers until brown all over and fish is cooked through. Serve skewers with rocket leaves.

KEBABS

3

DILL, CAPER AND LEMON

PREP + COOK TIME 30 MINUTES ♦ SERVES 4

Cut 750g (1½ pounds) ocean trout fillets into 2.5cm (1-inch) pieces. Combine fish with 1 clove crushed garlic, 2 teaspoons finely grated lemon rind, 2 tablespoons lemon juice, 1 tablespoon extra virgin olive oil, 1 tablespoon rinsed, drained chopped capers and 1 tablespoon chopped fresh dill in a large bowl. Thread fish onto 12 bamboo skewers; season. Preheat oiled grill plate (or grill or barbecue); cook skewers until brown all over and fish is cooked through. Serve skewers with coleslaw.

4

GINGER, SOY AND CORIANDER

PREP + COOK TIME 30 MINUTES ♦ SERVES 4

Combine 750g (1½ pounds) uncooked prawns, peeled with tails intact, with 2 teaspoons finely grated ginger, 1 tablespoon light soy sauce, 2 teaspoons peanut oil and 1 tablespoon coarsely chopped fresh coriander in a large bowl. Thread prawns onto 12 bamboo skewers; season. Preheat oiled grill plate (or grill or barbecue); cook skewers until brown all over and prawns are cooked through. Serve skewers with a cucumber and chilli salad.

1

BABY SPINACH AND PARMESAN SALAD

PREP TIME 10 MINUTES ◆ SERVES 4

Place 100g (3 ounces) baby spinach leaves, 50g (1½ ounces) shaved parmesan and 1 tablespoon toasted pine nuts in a large bowl. Combine 2 tablespoons balsamic vinegar and 1 tablespoon olive oil in a screw-top jar; shake well, season to taste. Drizzle dressing over salad; toss gently to combine.

2

BEAN AND TOMATO SALAD WITH HAZELNUT DRESSING

PREP + COOK TIME 20 MINUTES ◆ SERVES 4

Combine ½ cup roasted, skinned, coarsely chopped hazelnuts, 2 tablespoons each hazelnut oil and apple cider vinegar and 1 teaspoon wholegrain mustard in a screw-top jar; shake well. Boil, steam or microwave 200g (6½ ounces) trimmed green beans until tender; drain. Rinse under cold water; drain. Combine beans, 250g (8 ounces) quartered cherry tomatoes and hazelnut mixture in a medium bowl; toss gently to combine.

SALADS

3

OAK LEAF AND MIXED HERB SALAD WITH DIJON VINAIGRETTE

PREP TIME 10 MINUTES ◆ SERVES 6

Combine 2 tablespoons each olive oil and white wine vinegar with 1 tablespoon dijon mustard and 2 teaspoons white sugar in a screw-top jar; shake well. Combine dijon mixture with 1 green oak leaf lettuce, leaves separated, ¼ cup coarsely chopped fresh chives, ½ cup each firmly packed fresh flat-leaf parsley and fresh chervil leaves in a medium bowl; toss gently to combine.

4

COLESLAW

PREP TIME 15 MINUTES ◆ SERVES 4

Place 2 tablespoons mayonnaise and 1 tablespoon white wine vinegar in a screw-top jar; shake well. Place dressing in a large bowl with 2 cups finely shredded white cabbage, 1 cup finely shredded red cabbage, 1 coarsely grated medium carrot and 3 thinly sliced green onions; toss gently to combine.

WEEKEND

THE SLOWER PACE OF THE WEEKEND BRINGS WITH IT TIME TO COOK THE RECIPES THAT NEED MORE ATTENTION. IT'S THE PERFECT TIME FOR FAMILY FAVOURITES LIKE SLOW-COOKED ROASTS.

ZA'ATAR
IS A BLEND OF
ROASTED DRY HERBS,
SPICES, SESAME SEEDS AND
SALT. IT IS AVAILABLE FROM
MIDDLE-EASTERN FOOD SHOPS
AND SOME DELICATESSENS, OR
COMBINE 1 TABLESPOON EACH
SUMAC AND SESAME SEEDS
WITH 2 TEASPOONS FINELY
CHOPPED FRESH THYME
AND 1 TEASPOON
SALT.

ZA'ATAR-SPICED SCHNITZEL WITH FATTOUSH

PREP + COOK TIME 40 MINUTES ◆ SERVES 4

½ cup (35g) panko (japanese) breadcrumbs

2 tablespoons za'atar

2 teaspoons chopped fresh thyme

8 x 100g (3 ounces) veal scallopine (schnitzel)

⅓ cup (50g) plain (all-purpose) flour

2 eggs, beaten lightly

olive oil, for shallow-frying

FATTOUSH

2 large pitta breads (160g)

250g (8 ounces) cherry tomatoes, halved

2 lebanese cucumbers (260g), cut into ribbons

1 bunch red radishes, sliced thinly

3 green onions (scallions), sliced thinly

1 cup torn fresh flat-leaf parsley

½ cup fresh mint leaves

½ cup (125ml) olive oil

¼ cup (60ml) lemon juice

2 cloves garlic, crushed

1 To make fattoush, grill bread until crisp; break into small pieces. Combine tomato, cucumber, radish, onion and herbs in a large bowl. Just before serving, toss bread and combined oil, juice and garlic into salad. Season to taste.

2 Combine breadcrumbs, za'atar and thyme in a shallow bowl. Toss veal in flour, shake off excess. Dip in egg, then press on breadcrumb mixture to coat.

3 Heat oil in a large frying pan oven medium-high heat; cook veal for 2 minutes each side or until golden and cooked through.

4 Serve schnitzels with fattoush.

TEST KITCHEN NOTES

WE BOUGHT UNCRUMBED (PLAIN) SCHNITZELS TO USE IN THIS RECIPE.

LAMB, FETTA AND SPINACH PARCELS

PREP + COOK TIME 40 MINUTES ◆ SERVES 4

600g (1¼ pounds) trimmed spinach

300g (9½ ounces) fetta, crumbled

8 lamb fillets (1.5kg)

16 sheets fillo pastry

cooking-oil spray

250g (8 ounces) rocket (arugula)

½ small red onion (50g), sliced thinly

250g (8 ounces) baby roma (egg) tomatoes, halved

1 lebanese cucumber (130g), sliced thickly

2 tablespoons olive oil

1 tablespoon white balsamic vinegar

lemon wedges, to serve

1 Preheat oven to 240°C/475°F. Oil oven trays; line with baking paper.

2 Boil, steam or microwave spinach until tender; drain. Rinse under cold water; drain well, squeezing to remove any excess liquid. Chop spinach coarsely; combine in a medium bowl with fetta. Season.

3 Cook lamb, in batches, in a heated oiled large frying pan until browned. Cut lamb fillets in half.

4 To make fillo parcels, stack 4 fillo sheets, spraying individual sheets lightly with cooking oil. Cut stack in half widthways; cover with a slightly damp tea towel to prevent drying out. Repeat process with remaining 12 fillo sheets; you will have 8 fillo stacks.

5 Uncover one fillo stack; place on board. Centre two pieces of lamb on stack, top with an eighth of the spinach mixture. Roll stack to enclose filling, fold in sides after first complete turn. Spray parcel with cooking oil; place on tray. Repeat to make a total of 8 parcels.

6 Bake parcels for 15 minutes or until fillo is browned lightly.

7 Combine rocket, onion, tomato, cucumber, oil and vinegar in a medium bowl; season to taste. Serve parcels with salad; accompany with lemon wedges.

TEST KITCHEN NOTES

TO PREPARE PARCELS AHEAD OF TIME, MAKE SURE SPINACH HAS BEEN SQUEEZED OF ANY EXCESS LIQUID, OTHERWISE THE PASTRY WILL BECOME SOGGY. COVER PARCELS AND REFRIGERATE UNTIL READY TO BAKE.

SERVING SUGGESTION
YOU COULD ALSO SERVE PARCELS WITH A GREEK SALAD.

LAMB AND BEAN NACHOS WITH SALSA FRESCA

PREP + COOK TIME 40 MINUTES ◆ SERVES 4

1 tablespoon olive oil

500g (1 pound) minced (ground) lamb

1 clove garlic, crushed

1 teaspoon ground cumin

¼ teaspoon chilli powder

400g (12½ ounces) canned crushed tomatoes

425g (13½ ounces) canned Mexe beans, drained

¼ cup (60ml) water

240g (7½ ounces) plain toasted corn chips

1 cup (125g) coarsely grated cheddar

2 medium avocados (500g), mashed

½ cup (120g) sour cream

SALSA FRESCA

4 large roma (egg) tomatoes (360g), chopped finely

1 small red onion (100g), chopped finely

1 tablespoon olive oil

1 tablespoon lemon juice

1 clove garlic, crushed

2 tablespoons finely chopped fresh coriander (cilantro) leaves

1 Preheat oven to 180°C/350°F.

2 Heat oil in a large frying pan over high heat; cook lamb, garlic and spices, stirring, for 5 minutes or until browned. Add tomatoes, beans and the water; bring to the boil. Reduce heat to medium-low; simmer, uncovered, for 10 minutes or until lamb mixture thickens, stirring occasionally.

3 Just before serving, spread corn chips over a large heatproof plate; top with lamb mixture, sprinkle with cheddar. Bake nachos, uncovered, for 15 minutes or until heated through.

4 To make salsa fresca, combine ingredients in a medium bowl.

5 Combine avocado with half the salsa in a medium bowl; drop spoonfuls of the avocado mixture and sour cream over nachos. Top with remaining salsa.

TOMATO AND SPINACH STUFFED LAMB ROASTS

PREP + COOK TIME 35 MINUTES ◆ SERVES 4

½ cup (75g) drained, coarsely chopped sun-dried tomatoes

100g (3 ounces) fetta, crumbled

40g (1½ ounces) baby spinach leaves, chopped coarsely

2 mini lamb roasts (700g)

800g (1½ pounds) kumara (orange sweet potato), cut into wedges

2 tablespoons olive oil

6 sprigs fresh thyme

¼ teaspoon dried chilli flakes

1 Preheat oven to 200°C/400°F.

2 Combine tomato, fetta and spinach in a medium bowl.

3 Cut a horizontal pocket in each roast; do not cut all the way through. Press half the tomato mixture into each pocket; secure with toothpicks.

4 Heat an oiled small ovenproof frying pan over high heat. Cook lamb, turning, until browned all over.

5 Meanwhile, place kumara in a roasting pan, drizzle with oil and sprinkle with thyme and chilli; toss to combine. Season.

6 Transfer both pans to oven; roast, uncovered, for 20 minutes or until lamb is cooked as desired and kumara is golden and tender. Cover; stand 10 minutes.

7 Cut lamb into slices; serve with kumara wedges.

TEST KITCHEN NOTES

LAMB IS BEST STUFFED JUST BEFORE ROASTING; PREPARE THE TOMATO AND SPINACH FILLING AHEAD OF TIME AND STORE, COVERED, IN THE FRIDGE. ADD SOME CHILLI TO THE KUMARA FOR EXTRA FLAVOUR AND HEAT.

KIPFLER
POTATOES
ARE SMALL, FINGER-
SHAPED POTATOES
WITH A NUTTY
FLAVOUR; THEY'RE
GREAT BAKED.

LAMB RACK WITH HERB CRUST

PREP + COOK TIME 55 MINUTES ◆ SERVES 4

2 cloves garlic, quartered

¼ cup each loosely packed fresh basil, parsley and oregano leaves

¼ cup coarsely chopped fresh chives

1½ tablespoons olive oil

4 x 4 french-trimmed lamb cutlet racks (720g)

500g (1 pound) kipfler (fingerling) potatoes, scrubbed

1 tablespoon olive oil, extra

340g (11 ounces) asparagus, trimmed

lemon wedges, to serve

1 Preheat oven to 200°C/400°F.

2 Process garlic, herbs and oil until smooth.

3 Place lamb in a large shallow baking dish; press herb mixture onto each rack. Roast lamb, uncovered, for 20 minutes or until lamb is cooked as desired. Remove lamb from oven; cover, rest 10 minutes.

4 Meanwhile, microwave potatoes about 4 minutes. Toss potatoes and extra oil in a roasting pan, season to taste; roast about 15 minutes. Add asparagus to pan with potatoes and roast a further 10 minutes or until potatoes are golden and asparagus is tender.

5 Serve lamb with potatoes and asparagus; accompany with lemon wedges and extra oregano, if you like.

TEST KITCHEN NOTES

SUBSTITUTE WITH A COMBINATION OF YOUR FAVOURITE HERBS – FOR ASIAN-INSPIRED FLAVOURS TRY CORIANDER AND MINT. SERVE WITH ROASTED KUMARA (ORANGE SWEET POTATO).

PORK AND VEAL SANG CHOY BAU

PREP + COOK TIME 45 MINUTES ◆ SERVES 12

2 tablespoons peanut oil

1 large brown onion (200g), chopped finely

1 large carrot (180g), chopped finely

2 stalks celery (300g), trimmed, chopped finely

2 cloves garlic, crushed

2 teaspoons finely grated fresh ginger

750g (1½ pounds) minced (ground) pork and veal mixture

1 teaspoon sesame oil

¼ cup (60ml) oyster sauce

2 tablespoons sweet chilli sauce

2 tablespoons kecap manis

3 green onions (scallions), sliced thinly

12 butter (boston) lettuces leaves, from the middle of the lettuce

¼ cup (35g) coarsely chopped roasted peanuts

2 tablespoons fresh coriander (cilantro) leaves

1 Heat a wok over medium-high heat. Add peanut oil, onion, carrot, celery, garlic and ginger; stir-fry for 5 minutes or until just softened.

2 Add mince, stir-fry for 5 minutes, breaking up any lumps, or until browned. Stir in sesame oil and sauces for 3 minutes or until syrupy and heated through. Cool 10 minutes; stir in half the green onion.

3 To serve, spoon mixture into lettuce cups; top with peanuts, remaining green onion and coriander.

TEST KITCHEN NOTES

SOME SUPERMARKETS AND BUTCHERS SELL A PORK AND VEAL MINCE MIXTURE, WHICH IS WHAT WE USED HERE; IF THE MIXTURE IS NOT AVAILABLE, BUY HALF THE AMOUNT OF PORK MINCE AND HALF THE AMOUNT OF VEAL MINCE. ADD SOME FRESH MINT OR CORIANDER LEAVES TO THE MINCE MIXTURE.

BABY CARROTS
ARE ALSO SOLD AS
'DUTCH' CARROTS.
THEY ARE AVAILABLE
FROM SUPERMARKETS
AND GREENGROCERS.

PORK FILLET WITH APPLE AND LEEK

PREP + COOK TIME 35 MINUTES ◆ SERVES 4

800g (1½ pounds) pork fillets

¾ cup (180ml) chicken stock

2 medium leeks (700g), sliced thickly

1 clove garlic, crushed

2 tablespoons brown sugar

2 tablespoons red wine vinegar

10g (½ ounce) butter

2 medium apples (300g), unpeeled, sliced thinly

1 tablespoon brown sugar, extra

400g (12½ ounces) baby carrots, trimmed

250g (8 ounces) asparagus, trimmed, chopped coarsely

1 Preheat oven to 240°C/475°F.

2 Cook pork in a heated oiled frying pan, over medium-high heat, until browned all over. Place, in a single layer, in a large baking dish; bake, uncovered, for 20 minutes or until pork is cooked as desired. Cover; stand 5 minutes before slicing thickly.

3 Meanwhile, heat half the stock in a medium frying pan over medium-high heat; cook leek and garlic, stirring, for 10 minutes or until leek softens and browns slightly. Add sugar and vinegar; cook, stirring, for 5 minutes or until leek caramelises.

4 Add remaining stock to pan; bring to the boil. Reduce heat; simmer, uncovered, for 5 minutes or until liquid reduces by half. Place leek mixture in a medium bowl; cover to keep warm.

5 Melt butter in same pan over medium heat; cook apple and extra sugar, stirring, for 5 minutes or until apple is browned and tender.

6 Boil, steam or microwave carrot and asparagus, separately, until just tender; drain.

7 Serve pork with vegetables, caramelised apple and leek; season to taste.

TEST KITCHEN NOTES

PORK HAS A NATURAL AFFINITY WITH BOTH APPLE AND ONION; HERE, THESE TRADITIONAL ACCOMPANIMENTS ARE GIVEN A CONTEMPORARY TWIST. SERVE PORK WITH ANY STEAMED VEGETABLE THAT IS IN SEASON. THE LEEK MIXTURE CAN BE MADE SEVERAL HOURS AHEAD; STORE, COVERED, IN THE FRIDGE, REHEAT BEFORE SERVING.

BBQ PORK SPARE RIBS WITH CABBAGE SALAD

PREP + COOK TIME 45 MINUTES (+ REFRIGERATION) ◆ SERVES 4

1 cup (250ml) tomato sauce (ketchup)

¼ cup (60ml) worcestershire sauce

½ cup (110g) firmly packed brown sugar

2kg (4 pounds) American-style pork spare ribs

CABBAGE SALAD

¼ medium red cabbage (375g), shredded finely

¼ small green cabbage (300g), shredded finely

2 green onions (scallions), sliced thinly

⅓ cup (45g) toasted unsalted pistachios

½ cup loosely packed fresh flat-leaf parsley leaves

⅓ cup (80ml) honey mustard dressing

1 Combine sauces and sugar in a medium saucepan; bring to the boil. Remove from heat; cool marinade 10 minutes.

2 Place ribs in a large shallow baking dish, pour marinade all over pork; cover, refrigerate 3 hours or overnight, turning pork occasionally.

3 Drain ribs; reserve marinade. Cook ribs on a heated oiled grill plate (or grill or barbecue) for 30 minutes or until cooked through, turning and brushing frequently with some reserved marinade.

4 Meanwhile, to make cabbage salad, combine ingredients in a large bowl.

5 Boil remaining marinade in a small saucepan for 5 minutes or until thickened slightly.

6 Slice ribs into portions; serve with hot marinade and cabbage salad.

PORK WITH RATATOUILLE AND POTATOES

PREP + COOK TIME 1 HOUR ◆ SERVES 4

1kg (2 pounds) baby new (chat) potatoes, quartered

1 medium brown onion (150g), chopped coarsely

2 cloves garlic, crushed

4 baby eggplants (240g), sliced thickly

6 yellow patty-pan squash (180g), sliced thickly

400g (12½ ounces) canned crushed tomatoes

2 tablespoons finely shredded fresh basil leaves

4 x 150g (4½ ounces) pork steaks (medallions)

baby sorrel leaves, to serve

1 Preheat oven to 240°C/475°F.

2 Place potato in a large lightly oiled baking dish; roast, uncovered, for 25 minutes or until potato is browned and crisp.

3 Meanwhile, to make ratatouille, cook onion and garlic in a heated oiled frying pan over high heat, stirring, for 3 minutes or until onion softens. Add eggplant and squash; cook, stirring, for 5 minutes or until vegetables are tender.

4 Stir tomatoes into pan; bring to the boil. Reduce heat; simmer, uncovered, for 5 minutes or until vegetables are tender and sauce thickens. Stir basil into ratatouille; season to taste.

5 Cook pork, in batches, in a heated oiled frying pan over medium-high heat, for 4 minutes each side or until browned and cooked as desired.

6 Serve pork with potatoes and ratatouille; sprinkle with sorrel.

TEST KITCHEN NOTES

RATATOUILLE CAN BE MADE A DAY AHEAD; STORE, COVERED, IN THE FRIDGE. IT IS GREAT ON ITS OWN OR SERVED WITH PASTA.

IN CULINARY TERMS, 'JERK' REFERS TO A SPICY
JAMAICAN SEASONING USED TO MARINATE MEAT,
SEAFOOD OR POULTRY BEFORE GRILLING OR ROASTING.
WHILE EACH COOK HAS THEIR PARTICULAR FAVOURITE
COMBINATION OF SPICES, JERK ALMOST ALWAYS
CONTAINS ALLSPICE, THYME AND CHILLI.

JERK PORK CUTLETS WITH PUMPKIN CHIPS

PREP + COOK TIME 45 MINUTES ◆ SERVES 4

3 fresh long green chillies, chopped coarsely

3 green onions (scallions), chopped coarsely

2 cloves garlic, crushed

1 teaspoon ground allspice

1 teaspoon dried thyme

1 teaspoon white (granulated) sugar

1 tablespoon each light soy sauce and lime juice

4 x 280g pork loin chops

1kg (2-pound) piece pumpkin, trimmed

2 tablespoons vegetable oil

PIRI PIRI MAYONNAISE

⅓ cup (100g) mayonnaise

2 tablespoons piri piri sauce

1 Combine chilli, onion, garlic, allspice, thyme, sugar, sauce, juice and pork in a medium bowl.

2 To make piri piri mayonnaise, combine ingredients in a small bowl.

3 Cut pumpkin into 7cm (2¾-inch) chips; boil, steam or microwave until tender. Drain; combine chips with oil in a medium bowl. Cook chips on a heated oiled grill plate (or grill or barbecue) until browned.

4 Meanwhile, cook pork on a heated oiled grill plate (or grill or barbecue) for 4 minutes each side or until cooked through.

5 Serve pork with chips and piri piri mayonnaise.

**SERVING
SUGGESTION**
GREEN LEAFY
SALAD.

CHICKEN SALTIMBOCCA

PREP + COOK TIME 45 MINUTES ◆ SERVES 4

150g (4½ ounces) mozzarella

4 chicken breast fillets (800g)

8 slices prosciutto (120g)

16 fresh sage leaves

500g (1 pound) baby new (chat) potatoes, halved

60g (2 ounces) butter

2 tablespoons olive oil

6 fresh sage leaves, extra

⅔ cup (160ml) dry white wine

⅔ cup (160ml) chicken stock

1 Cut mozzarella into 8 even slices. Cut chicken fillets in half horizontally. Top each chicken piece with a slice of mozzarella, a slice of prosciutto and 2 sage leaves, securing sage to prosciutto with a toothpick.

2 Cook potato in a saucepan of boiling salted water about 4 minutes to par-boil. Drain.

3 Heat half the butter and half the oil in a large frying pan. Cook potato and extra sage for 2 minutes or until golden. Season; transfer to a bowl to keep warm.

4 Heat remaining oil in same pan over medium heat; cook chicken, sage-side down first, in two batches, for 3 minutes each side or until cooked through. Remove from pan; cover to keep warm.

5 Add remaining butter, wine and stock to same pan, bring to the boil; reduce heat, simmer, stirring, for 5 minutes or until liquid reduces slightly. Season.

6 Serve chicken with sauce and potato.

TEST KITCHEN NOTES

SALTIMBOCCA IS ITALIAN FOR 'JUMPS IN THE MOUTH'. THE CHEESE WILL MAKE THE PROSCIUTTO STICK TO THE CHICKEN. REMOVE THE TOOTHPICKS BEFORE SERVING. THIS DISH GOES WELL WITH A GREEN SALAD FOR LUNCH OR WITH STEAMED OR ROASTED VEGETABLES FOR DINNER.

CHICKEN AND ASPARAGUS RAVIOLI

PREP + COOK TIME 45 MINUTES ◆ SERVES 4

250g (8 ounces) asparagus, trimmed

200g (6½ ounces) minced (ground) chicken

2 teaspoons olive oil

270g (8½-ounce) packet wonton wrappers

1 egg, beaten lightly

1 medium lemon (140g)

125g (4 ounces) butter

1 clove garlic, crushed

2 tablespoons fresh chervil

1 Boil, steam or microwave asparagus until just tender; drain. Halve asparagus, reserve tops; coarsely chop stalks.

2 Combine chicken, oil and asparagus stalks in a medium bowl; season.

3 Brush wonton wrapper with egg. Place 1 rounded teaspoon of chicken mixture in centre of wrapper; top with another wrapper, press edges together to seal. Repeat with remaining wrappers, egg and chicken mixture.

4 Using a vegetable peeler, thinly peel rind from lemon. Cut rind into narrow strips. Squeeze juice from lemon (you will need 2 tablespoons of juice).

5 Cook ravioli, in batches, in a large saucepan of boiling water, for 5 minutes or until chicken is cooked through; drain. Divide into bowls, top with reserved asparagus.

6 Heat butter in a medium frying pan over medium heat; cook until butter turns a nut-brown colour. Immediately add garlic, then juice; season. Pour sauce over ravioli; sprinkle with chervil. Serve with grated parmesan, if you like.

TEST KITCHEN NOTES

USING PACKAGED WONTON WRAPPERS MAKES THIS DISH MUCH EASIER TO ASSEMBLE. WHILE THE RAVIOLI ARE COOKING, STIR OCCASIONALLY TO PREVENT THEM FROM STICKING TOGETHER.

CHERVIL IS A CURLY LEAFED HERB WITH A MILD FENNEL FLAVOUR. SUBSTITUTE WITH FLAT-LEAF PARSLEY.

SERVING SUGGESTION
GREEN LEAFY SALAD.

PAPRIKA CHICKEN WITH TOMATO AND CHICKPEAS

PREP + COOK TIME 1 HOUR 15 MINUTES (+ REFRIGERATION) ◆ SERVES 4

4 chicken marylands (1.4kg)

1 tablespoon ground turmeric

2 teaspoons smoked paprika

2 teaspoons finely grated lemon rind

1 clove garlic, crushed

⅓ cup (80ml) olive oil

500g (1 pound) cherry truss tomatoes on the vine

400g (12½ ounces) canned chickpeas (garbanzo beans), rinsed, drained

⅓ cup fresh flat-leaf parsley leaves

1 tablespoon lemon juice

1 Using a knife, cut three slashes widthways into each maryland.

2 Combine chicken, turmeric, paprika, rind, garlic and half the oil in a large bowl. Cover; refrigerate 3 hours or overnight.

3 Preheat oven to 220°C/425°F. Line a roasting pan with baking paper.

4 Place chicken, in a single layer, on a wire rack over a baking dish; roast, uncovered, for 45 minutes or until chicken is tender.

5 Combine tomatoes and half the remaining oil in a small baking dish; roast, uncovered, in oven with the chicken, for 15 minutes or until just tender.

6 Just before serving, add chickpeas, parsley, juice and remaining oil to tomatoes.

TEST KITCHEN NOTES

INSTEAD OF MARYLANDS, USE CHICKEN CUTLETS OR DRUMSTICKS. MARINATED CHICKEN CAN BE FROZEN FOR UP TO 3 MONTHS; DEFROST OVERNIGHT IN THE FRIDGE.

MUSTARD ROSEMARY CHICKEN

PREP + COOK TIME 25 MINUTES (+ REFRIGERATION) ◆ SERVES 4

2 tablespoons lemon juice

¼ cup (60ml) olive oil

2 cloves garlic, crushed

2 tablespoons finely chopped fresh rosemary

¼ cup (60g) wholegrain mustard

8 chicken thigh cutlets (1.2kg)

½ cup (125ml) dry white wine

300ml pouring cream

1 teaspoon cornflour (cornstarch)

1 teaspoon water

1 bunch mixed heirloom baby carrots (400g), trimmed, peeled

200g (6½ ounces) baby green beans

1 tablespoon finely chopped fresh rosemary, extra

1 Combine juice, oil, garlic, rosemary, mustard and chicken in a medium bowl, cover; refrigerate 3 hours or overnight.

2 Drain chicken over a small bowl; reserve marinade. Cook chicken on a heated oiled grill plate (or grill or barbecue) for 10 minutes or until browned all over and cooked through.

3 Meanwhile, place reserved marinade and wine in a small saucepan, bring to the boil; boil for 5 minutes or until reduced by half. Stir in cream, then blended cornflour and the water; bring to the boil, stirring, until mixture thickens slightly.

4 Boil, steam or microwave carrots and beans, separately, until tender.

5 Serve chicken with vegetables; drizzle with sauce and sprinkle with extra rosemary. Accompany with crusty bread, if you like.

TEST KITCHEN NOTES

WE USED A SEMILLON-STYLE WINE, BUT YOU CAN USE YOUR FAVOURITE DRY WHITE WINE.

HEIRLOOM BABY CARROTS ARE A COLOURFUL MIX OF PURPLE, ORANGE AND YELLOW BABY CARROTS. THEY ARE AVAILABLE FROM SOME GREENGROCERS AND SUPERMARKETS.

CHILLI-COCONUT PRAWNS

PREP + COOK TIME 45 MINUTES ◆ SERVES 4

⅔ cup (130g) white long-grain rice

750g (1½ pounds) medium uncooked king prawns (shrimp)

1 tablespoon peanut oil

1 large brown onion (200g), sliced thinly

2 cloves garlic, crushed

2 teaspoons finely grated fresh ginger

1 tablespoon each black mustard seeds, ground cumin and ground coriander

2 fresh small red thai (serrano) chillies, chopped finely

8 fresh curry leaves, torn

400ml canned coconut cream

½ cup (125ml) water

1 bunch (500g) choy sum, chopped coarsely

2 tablespoons fresh coriander (cilantro) leaves

1 Cook rice according to packet directions until tender. Cover to keep warm.

2 Meanwhile, shell and devein prawns, leaving tails intact.

3 Heat oil in a wok over high heat; stir-fry onion, garlic and ginger for 3 minutes or until onion is soft. Add seeds, cumin, coriander, chilli and curry leaves; cook, stirring, until seeds pop.

4 Add combined coconut cream and the water. Bring to the boil, then simmer, uncovered, for 5 minutes or until sauce thickens. Add prawns and choy sum; simmer, uncovered, for 5 minutes or until prawns change colour and are just cooked.

5 Serve prawns with rice; sprinkle with coriander.

TEST KITCHEN NOTES

BUY SHELLED PRAWNS WITH THE TAILS INTACT FROM THE FROZEN SECTION IN SUPERMARKETS; DEFROST IN THE FRIDGE BEFORE COOKING. SERVE WITH STEAMED ASIAN GREENS, IF YOU LIKE.

CAJUN-SPICED FISH WITH ROASTED CORN SALAD

PREP + COOK TIME 35 MINUTES ◆ SERVES 4

1 clove garlic, crushed

1 tablespoon butter, melted

2 teaspoons sweet paprika

½ teaspoon ground cumin

1 teaspoon ground white pepper

¼ teaspoon cayenne pepper

4 x 200g (6½ ounces) firm white fish fillets

3 trimmed corn cobs (750g)

1 small red onion (100g), chopped coarsely

1 medium avocado (250g), chopped coarsely

250g (8 ounces) cherry tomatoes, halved

2 tablespoons lime juice

¼ cup coarsely chopped fresh coriander (cilantro)

1 Preheat oven to 200°C/400°F.

2 Combine garlic and butter in a small jug; combine spices in a small bowl.

3 Place fish on an oven tray; brush both sides with garlic mixture, sprinkle with combined spices. Roast, uncovered, for 15 minutes, turning halfway through cooking time, or until browned both sides and cooked as desired.

4 Meanwhile, roast corn on a heated lightly oiled grill plate (or grill or barbecue) for 10 minutes or until browned all over. When corn is just cool enough to handle, cut kernels from cobs with a small, sharp knife.

5 Combine corn in a medium bowl with remaining ingredients. Serve fish with salsa and accompany with warmed flour tortillas, if you like.

TEST KITCHEN NOTES

WE USED BLUE-EYE (TREVALLY) IN THIS RECIPE, BUT YOU CAN USE ANY FIRM WHITE FISH FILLETS.

VEGETARIAN OYSTER SAUCE
IS MADE FROM BLENDED MUSHROOMS AND SOY SAUCE. IT IS AVAILABLE FROM HEALTH FOOD STORES AND SOME SUPERMARKETS.

TOFU AND SUGAR SNAP PEA STIR-FRY

PREP + COOK TIME 40 MINUTES (+ STANDING) ◆ SERVES 4

600g (1½ pounds) firm tofu

⅔ cup (130g) white long-grain rice

1 tablespoon sesame oil

1 large red onion (300g), sliced thickly

2 cloves garlic, crushed

2 teaspoons finely grated fresh ginger

1 teaspoon cornflour (cornstarch)

⅓ cup (80ml) soy sauce

200g (6½ ounces) sugar snap peas, trimmed

350g (11 ounces) baby buk choy, chopped lengthways

1 tablespoon brown sugar

⅓ cup (80ml) vegetarian oyster sauce

2 tablespoons mirin

¼ cup fresh coriander (cilantro) leaves

1 Preheat oven to 200°C/400°F.

2 Weight tofu between two boards; stand, tilted, for 10 minutes to remove excess liquid. Cut tofu into 2cm (¾-inch) cubes; pat dry between layers of paper towel. Place tofu on baking-paper-lined oven trays. Bake, uncovered, for 10 minutes or until browned lightly.

3 Meanwhile, cook rice according to packet directions until tender.

4 Heat oil in a wok over high heat; stir-fry onion, garlic and ginger for 3 minutes or until onion softens. Add blended cornflour and soy sauce to wok with tofu, peas, buk choy, sugar, oyster sauce and mirin; stir-fry until sauce boils and thickens slightly. Remove from heat, stir in coriander; serve with rice.

TEST KITCHEN NOTES

BUY THE SMALLEST BABY BUK CHOY YOU CAN FIND. YOU COULD ALSO USE GAI LAN OR TA GHO (AVAILABLE FROM ASIAN GREENGROCERS). IF YOU CAN'T FIND MIRIN USE SWEET WHITE WINE OR SHERRY, INSTEAD.

FELAFEL WRAPS

PREP + COOK TIME 45 MINUTES (+ REFRIGERATION) ◆ SERVES 4

¾ cup (110g) frozen broad beans (fava beans), thawed, peeled

400g (12½ ounces) canned chickpeas (garbanzo beans), rinsed, drained

⅓ cup coarsely chopped fresh flat-leaf parsley

1 small red onion (100g), chopped coarsely

⅓ cup (50g) plain (all-purpose) flour

2 teaspoons ground coriander

1 teaspoon ground cumin

1 egg

4 large pitta breads (320g)

1 cup (260g) hummus

50g (1½ ounces) mesclun

125g (4 ounces) cherry tomatoes, halved

MARINATED GRILLED EGGPLANT

6 baby eggplants (360g), sliced thinly lengthways

2 tablespoons olive oil

2 cloves garlic, crushed

1 tablespoon white wine vinegar

2 tablespoons finely chopped fresh flat-leaf parsley

1 Blend or process beans, chickpeas, parsley, onion, flour, spices and egg until almost smooth. Shape rounded tablespoons of the mixture into 16 felafel patties. Place on a tray, cover; refrigerate 30 minutes.

2 Meanwhile, to make marinated grilled eggplant, cook eggplant on a heated oiled flat plate (or in a frying pan) over medium heat for 4 minutes or until browned lightly both sides. Combine eggplant in a medium bowl with remaining ingredients.

3 Cook felafel on a heated oiled flat plate (or in a frying pan) over medium heat, for 4 minutes each side or until browned and heated through.

4 Spread pittas with hummus; top with mesclun, eggplant, tomato and felafel; roll to enclose filling. Serve with grilled lemons, if you like.

TEST KITCHEN NOTES

TO SAVE TIME, USE CHAR-GRILLED EGGPLANT FROM THE DELI.

ANTIPASTO TARTS

PREP + COOK TIME 40 MINUTES ◆ SERVES 4

¼ cup (60ml) olive oil

2 cloves garlic, crushed

1 small red capsicum (bell pepper) (150g), chopped coarsely

1 small yellow capsicum (bell pepper) (150g), chopped coarsely

1 medium zucchini (120g), sliced thinly

2 baby eggplants (120g), sliced thinly

1 small red onion (100g), sliced thickly

200g (6½ ounces) grape tomatoes

150g (4½ ounces) baby bocconcini cheese, halved

½ cup (40g) finely grated parmesan

½ cup firmly packed fresh basil leaves

2 sheets ready-rolled puff pastry

⅓ cup (85g) bottled tomato pasta sauce

¼ cup pitted black olives, torn

2 tablespoons baby basil leaves

150g (4½ ounces) mixed salad leaves

1 Preheat oven to 200°C/400°F.

2 Combine oil and garlic in a large bowl. Add capsicums, zucchini, eggplant and onion; toss gently to coat vegetables in mixture, season.

3 Cook vegetables, in batches, on a heated oiled grill plate (or grill or barbecue) until browned lightly and just tender; return to bowl. Add tomato, cheeses and basil; toss gently to combine.

4 Cut pastry sheets in half; fold edges 1cm (½-inch) inward, place on oiled oven trays. Divide sauce among pastry pieces; top with vegetable mixture. Bake for 15 minutes or until pastry has browned lightly.

5 Top tarts with olives; sprinkle with baby basil and serve with salad leaves.

CLASSIC LAMB BURRITO

PREP + COOK TIME 30 MINUTES ◆ SERVES 4

500g (1 pound) minced (ground) lamb

35g (1-ounce) packet taco seasoning mix

400g (12½ ounces) canned crushed tomatoes

425g (13 ounces) canned Mexe beans

¼ cup (60ml) water

4 x 20cm (8-inch) flour tortillas, warmed

1 cup shredded iceberg lettuce

1 medium tomato (150g), chopped coarsely

¾ cup (90g) grated tasty cheese

1 Cook lamb in a heated oiled pan for 5 minutes or until browned.

2 Add seasoning mix, tomatoes, beans and the water to pan; boil then reduce heat to medium-low. Simmer, uncovered, for 10 minutes or until mixture thickens; season.

3 Divide mixture between tortillas. Divide lettuce, tomato and cheese evenly over lamb mixture, fold to enclose filling.

PESTO, SUN-DRIED TOMATO AND CHICKEN PASTA

PREP + COOK TIME 25 MINUTES ◆ SERVES 4

375g (12 ounces) penne pasta

340g (11 ounces) semi-dried tomatoes in oil

⅓ cup (90g) bottled basil pesto

2 cups (320g) shredded barbecued chicken

2 tablespoons finely grated parmesan

1 Cook pasta in a large saucepan of boiling water until tender; drain, reserving ⅓ cup of the cooking liquid.

2 Meanwhile, drain tomatoes, reserving 2 tablespoons of the oil.

3 Return pasta to pan with pesto, chicken, tomatoes, reserved oil and cooking liquid. Stir gently until heated through. Sprinkle with parmesan to serve.

ASPARAGUS AND FETTA FRITTATA

PREP + COOK TIME 35 MINUTES (+ COOLING) ◆ SERVES 4

170g (5½ ounces) asparagus, trimmed, chopped coarsely

2 small zucchini (180g), sliced thinly lengthways

1 cup (120g) frozen peas

8 eggs

½ cup (125ml) pouring cream

½ cup lightly packed fresh mint leaves, torn

150g (4½ ounces) fetta, crumbled

1 Preheat oven to 180°C/350°F. Oil a 20cm x 30cm (8-inch x 12-inch) rectangular pan; line base with baking paper, extending the paper 5cm (2 inches) over the long sides.

2 Place asparagus, zucchini and peas in a small saucepan of boiling water. Return to the boil; drain immediately, transfer to a bowl of iced water until cold. Drain well, then pat dry with paper towel.

3 Whisk eggs and cream in a large jug until combined. Add mint; season.

4 Place fetta and vegetables in pan; pour over egg mixture.

5 Bake for 25 minutes or until set. Cool before cutting frittata into slices.

TEST KITCHEN NOTES

STORE COOLED FRITTATA, COVERED, IN REFRIGERATOR FOR UP TO 2 DAYS. YOU CAN ALSO START COOKING FRITTATA IN A NON-STICK OVENPROOF FRYING PAN ON THE STOVE TOP AND FINISH IT UNDER THE GRILL (BROILER). FRITTATA CAN BE EATEN WARM OR AT ROOM TEMPERATURE.

1

RICOTTA AND BASIL

PREP + COOK TIME 15 MINUTES ◆ MAKES 2

Preheat oven to 220°C/425°F. Oil two oven trays or pizza pans. Place 2 large pitta breads or store-bought pizza bases on oven trays; spread with ⅔ cup tomato pasta sauce, top with ½ cup crumbled firm ricotta. Bake for 10 minutes or until bases are crisp. Top with 1 cup loosely packed basil leaves to serve.

2

SALAMI AND CAPSICUM

PREP + COOK TIME 20 MINUTES ◆ MAKES 2

Preheat oven to 220°C/425°F. Oil two oven trays or pizza pans. Place 2 large pitta breads or store-bought pizza bases on oven trays; spread with ⅔ cup tomato pasta sauce, top with 1½ cups coarsely grated mozzarella, 125g (4 ounces) thinly sliced salami and 85g (3 ounces) thinly sliced roasted red capsicum. Bake for 15 minutes or until bases are crisp. Sprinkle with ¼ cup loosely packed fresh basil leaves to serve.

PIZZA

3

PUMPKIN AND FETTA

PREP + COOK TIME 20 MINUTES ◆ MAKES 2

Preheat oven to 220°C/425°F. Oil two oven trays or pizza pans. Using a vegetable peeler, slice a 200g (6½ ounces) piece pumpkin into thin strips. Place 2 large pitta breads or store-bought pizza bases on oven trays; spread with ⅔ cup tomato pasta sauce, then top with pumpkin. Spray with cooking oil; sprinkle with 100g (3 ounces) crumbled fetta. Bake for 10 minutes or until pumpkin is tender and bases are crisp. Top with 50g (1½ ounces) rocket (arugula) to serve.

4

CHICKEN AND MUSHROOM

PREP + COOK TIME 20 MINUTES ◆ MAKES 2

Preheat oven to 220°C/425°F. Oil two oven trays or pizza pans. Place 2 large pitta breads or store-bought pizza bases on oven trays; spread with ⅔ cup tomato pasta sauce, top with 2 cups shredded barbecued chicken, 100g (3 ounces) halved button mushrooms and ½ cup pizza cheese. Bake for 15 minutes or until bases are crisp. Sprinkle with ⅓ cup loosely packed fresh flat-leaf parsley leaves to serve.

1
SAUTÉED POTATOES

PREP + COOK TIME 20 MINUTES ◆ SERVES 4

Cut 1kg (2 pounds) unpeeled desiree potatoes into 1cm (½-inch) slices. Heat 2 tablespoons olive oil and 50g (1½ ounces) chopped butter in a large frying pan; cook potato, covered, over medium-low heat, turning occasionally, for 10 minutes or until browned lightly and tender.

TIPS

Sautéed potatoes are quick and easy to make. You can also use ghee, unsalted butter or a mixture of butter and oil, if you prefer, because all can be used over high heat without burning. You can also use sebago potatoes for this recipe.

2
LYONNAISE POTATOES

PREP + COOK TIME 30 MINUTES ◆ SERVES 4

Boil, steam or microwave 900g (1¾ pounds) coarsely chopped peeled desiree potatoes until just tender; drain. Meanwhile, heat 2 teaspoons olive oil in a large frying pan; cook 2 thinly sliced medium red onions and 3 cloves crushed garlic, stirring, until onion softens. Remove from pan. Cook 6 coarsely chopped rindless bacon slices in the same pan, stirring, until crisp; drain on paper towel. Heat an extra 2 teaspoons olive oil in same pan; cook potato, stirring, for 5 minutes or until browned lightly. Return onion mixture and bacon to pan; stir gently to combine with potato. Remove from heat; stir in ¼ cup coarsely chopped fresh mint.

POTATO

3
POTATO SALAD WITH HERBED CREAM

PREP + COOK TIME 25 MINUTES ◆ SERVES 8

To make herbed cream, combine ½ cup each mayonnaise and sour cream, ¼ cup warm water, 3 teaspoons dijon mustard, ¼ cup finely chopped fresh chives and ½ cup coarsely chopped fresh flat-leaf parsley in a screw-top jar; shake well. Boil, steam or microwave 1.5kg (3 pounds) scrubbed, unpeeled medium kipfler potatoes until tender; drain. Cool, then slice potatoes crossways into 2cm (¾-inch) thick rounds. Drizzle potato with herbed cream.

4
THE PERFECT RÖSTI

PREP + COOK TIME 25 MINUTES ◆ MAKES 8

Grate 1kg (2 pounds) potatoes coarsely into a large bowl, stir in 1 teaspoon salt; squeeze excess moisture from potatoes. Divide potato mixture into eight portions. Heat 10g (½ ounce) butter and 1 teaspoon vegetable oil in a medium frying pan; spread one portion of the potato mixture over base of pan, flatten with a spatula or egg slice to form a firm pancake. Cook, uncovered, over medium heat, until golden brown on the underside; shake pan to loosen rösti, then invert onto a large plate. Gently slide rösti back into pan; cook, uncovered, until other side is golden brown and potato centre is tender. Drain on paper towel; cover to keep warm. Repeat to make a total of eight rösti.

COMFORT

SNUGGLE UP WITH A BOWL OF PIPING HOT BOLOGNESE, FRESH-FROM-THE-PAN RISOTTO OR YOUR VERY OWN PIE TOPPED WITH FLAKY PASTRY. THERE'S ALWAYS AN EXCUSE FOR FAMILY COMFORT FOOD.

SERVING SUGGESTION PAN-FRIED BABY CARROTS, STEAMED ASPARAGUS OR BROCCOLI.

STEAK BOURGUIGNON WITH CELERIAC POTATO MASH

PREP + COOK TIME 40 MINUTES ◆ SERVES 4

1 small celeriac (400g), chopped coarsely

2 medium potatoes (400g), chopped coarsely

¼ cup (60ml) milk

40g (1½ ounces) butter

cooking-oil spray

4 x 200g (6½ ounces) beef eye-fillet steaks

200g (6½ ounces) button mushrooms, halved

6 baby onions (150g), quartered

2 cloves garlic, crushed

½ cup (125ml) dry red wine

1 cup (250ml) beef stock

1 tablespoon tomato paste

1 tablespoon coarsely chopped fresh thyme

1 Boil, steam or microwave celeriac and potato, separately, until tender; drain. Mash in a medium bowl with milk and butter; cover to keep warm.

2 Meanwhile, spray a large frying pan with cooking oil; heat over medium-high heat. Cook beef for 4 minutes each side or until browned and cooked as desired; remove from pan, cover to keep warm.

3 Cook mushrooms, onion and garlic in same pan until vegetables just soften. Add wine, stock and paste; simmer, uncovered, for 5 minutes or until sauce thickens slightly.

4 Serve beef with mash and bourguignon sauce; sprinkle with thyme.

TEST KITCHEN NOTES

MASH CAN BE MADE A DAY AHEAD; STORE, COVERED, IN THE FRIDGE. REHEAT JUST BEFORE SERVING. YOU CAN SUBSTITUTE RIB-EYE (SCOTCH FILLET) OR SIRLOIN (NEW-YORK CUT) STEAK FOR EYE-FILLET. RECIPE IS NOT SUITABLE TO FREEZE.

BEEF AND MUSHROOM POT PIES

PREP + COOK TIME 30 MINUTES ◆ SERVES 4

1 sheet ready-rolled puff pastry

1 tablespoon olive oil

1 medium brown onion (150g), sliced thinly

1 clove garlic, crushed

250g (8 ounces) button mushrooms, quartered

500g (1 pound) beef rump steak, trimmed, sliced thinly

1 tablespoon plain (all-purpose) flour

½ cup (125ml) dry red wine

½ cup (125ml) beef stock

400g (12½ ounces) canned crushed tomatoes

2 tablespoons tomato paste

2 teaspoons fresh thyme leaves

1 Preheat oven to 200°C/400°F.

2 Cut pastry sheet into four squares.

3 Heat oil in a large frying pan over medium-high heat; cook onion and garlic, stirring, for 4 minutes or until onion softens. Add mushrooms; cook, stirring, about 2 minutes.

4 Toss beef with flour in a medium bowl, add to pan; cook, stirring, for 5 minutes or until beef is browned. Stir in wine, stock, tomatoes and paste; bring to the boil. Reduce heat to low; simmer, uncovered, for 10 minutes or until mixture thickens slightly. Stir in thyme.

5 Spoon beef mixture into 4 x 1-cup (250ml) square ramekins. Place pastry over each dish, securing with a little water; carefully cut a hole in the top of each pastry square. Bake for 15 minutes or until pastry is puffed and browned.

TEST KITCHEN NOTES

IF YOU HAVE A PIE MAKER CUT THE PASTRY ACCORDING TO THE INSTRUCTIONS AND COOK IN THE PIE MAKER UNTIL GOLDEN BROWN. WE USED A SHIRAZ-STYLE WINE IN THIS RECIPE, YOU CAN USE ANY RED YOU HAVE OPEN.

SERVING SUGGESTION
SERVE PIES WITH SMASHED PEA AND POTATO MASH: COMBINE A 476G (15-OUNCE) TUB MASHED POTATO WITH 2 CUPS SMASHED STEAMED PEAS AND 40G (1½ OUNCES) MELTED BUTTER.

COTTAGE PIE

PREP + COOK TIME 1 HOUR 30 MINUTES ♦ SERVES 4

2 teaspoons olive oil

1kg (2 pounds) minced (ground) beef

1 medium brown onion (150g), chopped finely

1 medium carrot (120g), sliced finely

1 trimmed celery stalk (100g), sliced finely

1 tablespoon chopped fresh thyme leaves

1 cup (250ml) beef stock

1 tablespoon worcestershire sauce

¼ cup (70g) tomato paste

400g (12½ ounces) canned diced tomatoes

½ cup (60g) frozen peas

2 tablespoons grated cheddar

POTATO TOPPING

6 medium potatoes (1.2kg), chopped coarsely

60g (2 ounces) butter

¼ cup (60ml) milk

1 Preheat oven to 180°C/350°F.

2 Heat oil in a large saucepan over high heat; cook beef and onion, stirring, for 5 minutes or until browned.

3 Add carrot, celery, thyme, stock, sauce, paste and tomatoes; simmer, uncovered, for 30 minutes or until carrots are tender. Add peas; cook for 10 minutes or until peas are tender and the liquid has thickened.

4 Meanwhile, to make potato topping, boil, steam or microwave potato until tender; drain. Mash potato with butter and milk.

5 Spoon beef mixture into a 2.5-litre (10-cup) ovenproof dish. Spread potato topping over beef mixture; sprinkle with cheddar. Bake, uncovered, for 30 minutes or until pie is heated through and topping is golden. Serve sprinkled with extra thyme, if you like.

MUSTARD VEAL WITH POLENTA AND SPINACH PUREE

PREP + COOK TIME 35 MINUTES ◆ SERVES 4

⅓ cup (95g) wholegrain mustard

2 tablespoons coarsely chopped fresh oregano

4 cloves garlic

8 veal chops (1.5kg)

350g (11 ounces) truss cherry tomatoes

2 cups (500ml) water

1 teaspoon salt

1 cup (170g) polenta

¾ cup (180ml) milk

¼ cup (20g) finely grated parmesan

350g (11 ounces) spinach, trimmed

1 anchovy fillet, drained

1 tablespoon lemon juice

1 cup (250ml) beef stock

1 Preheat oven to 180°C/350°F.

2 Meanwhile, place grill shelf on the low rung. Preheat grill (broiler) to medium-high heat.

3 Combine mustard, oregano and 2 crushed garlic cloves in a small bowl; brush veal both sides with mixture. Cook veal under grill until browned both sides and cooked as desired.

4 Meanwhile, cook tomatoes on a baking-paper-lined oven tray, in oven, for 10 minutes or until softened.

5 Combine the water and salt in a medium saucepan; bring to the boil. Stir in polenta, reduce heat to low; cook, stirring, for 10 minutes or until polenta thickens. Stir in milk; cook, stirring, for 5 minutes or until polenta thickens. Stir in parmesan; season to taste.

6 Boil, steam or microwave spinach until just wilted. When cool enough to handle, squeeze out excess liquid with hands. Crush remaining garlic. Blend or process spinach with garlic and remaining ingredients until pureed.

7 Serve veal with tomato, accompany with polenta and spinach mixture; sprinkle with extra oregano leaves before serving, if you like.

TEST KITCHEN NOTES

POLENTA IS THE ITALIAN ANSWER TO MASHED POTATO - IT'S THE PERFECT ACCOMPANIMENT FOR SOAKING UP MEAT JUICES AND TOO-GOOD-TO-WASTE SAUCES. IT IS AVAILABLE IN REGULAR AND INSTANT FROM SUPERMARKETS.

SERVING
SUGGESTION

RADICCHIO OR ROCKET
SALAD DRESSED WITH
BALSAMIC VINEGAR.

FRESH ROSEMARY
OR THYME CAN BE
SUBSTITUTED FOR
OREGANO.

SERVING
SUGGESTION
STEAMED GREENS
SUCH AS PEAS,
BROCCOLINI AND
BEANS SPRINKLED
WITH 1 TABLESPOON
BABY MINT
LEAVES.

BAKED LAMB CHOPS WITH CAPSICUM AND TOMATO

PREP + COOK TIME 45 MINUTES ◆ SERVES 4

4 lamb forequarter chops (760g)

2 medium yellow capsicums (bell pepper) (400g), sliced thickly

375g (12 ounces) cherry truss tomatoes on the vine

1 small red onion (100g), cut into wedges

2 x 475g (15-ounce) tubs mashed potato

1 Preheat oven to 200°C/400°F.

2 Heat a large flameproof baking dish over high heat. Cook lamb until browned all over. Add capsicum, tomato and onion to dish.

3 Transfer dish to oven; roast, uncovered, for 30 minutes or until lamb is cooked through and vegetables are tender.

4 Microwave mashed potato according to directions on tub.

5 Serve lamb with vegetables and mashed potato.

TEST KITCHEN NOTES

WE USED PREPARED MASHED POTATO, AVAILABLE FROM THE REFRIGERATED SECTION AT SUPERMARKETS.

GINGER-CHILLI PORK SPARE RIBS

PREP + COOK TIME 1 HOUR 45 MINUTES ◆ SERVES 4

1.5kg (3 pounds) pork spare ribs

6cm (2½-inch) piece fresh ginger (35g), cut into matchsticks

¼ cup (60ml) dry sherry

2 teaspoons sambal oelek

½ cup (125ml) water

1 tablespoon dark soy sauce

1 tablespoon black bean sauce

2 tablespoons caster (superfine) sugar

2 tablespoons honey

1 bunch choy sum (400g)

450g (14½-ounce) packet microwave jasmine rice

1 Place ribs in a large saucepan of boiling water, simmer, uncovered, about 15 minutes; drain, cool.

2 Combine ginger in a small bowl with sherry, sambal, the water, sauces, sugar and honey; mix well.

3 Preheat oven to 220°C/425°F. Line a roasting pan with baking paper.

4 Place ribs in pan, add ginger mixture; roast, covered, about 45 minutes. Uncover, roast a further 25 minutes or until ribs are tender and well browned. Remove from pan. Simmer sauce in pan, uncovered, until very thick.

5 Meanwhile, boil, steam or microwave choy sum until just wilted. Microwave rice according to directions on packet.

6 Serve ribs with choy sum and rice; drizzle with warm sauce.

TEST KITCHEN NOTES

SUBSTITUTE SAMBAL OELEK WITH 1 FINELY CHOPPED FRESH LONG RED CHILLI. RECIPE CAN BE MADE A DAY AHEAD; STORE, COVERED, IN THE FRIDGE.

SERVING
SUGGESTION
ACCOMPANY WITH
SEEDED BREAD
ROLLS.

BAKED PASTA WITH HAM, BLUE CHEESE AND FENNEL

PREP + COOK TIME 45 MINUTES ◆ SERVES 4

375g (12 ounces) shell pasta

250g (8 ounces) ham, sliced thinly

4 eggs, beaten lightly

300ml pouring cream

½ cup (125ml) milk

200g (6½ ounces) soft blue cheese, crumbled

2 small fennel bulbs (400g), trimmed, sliced thinly, fennel fronds reserved

¼ cup (20g) finely grated parmesan

250g (8 ounces) heirloom cherry tomatoes, halved or quartered

1 tablespoon olive oil

1 Preheat oven to 200°C/400°F.

2 Cook pasta in a large saucepan of boiling water until just tender; drain.

3 Meanwhile, cook ham in a small frying pan, over medium heat, stirring, for 2 minutes or until browned.

4 Combine ham and pasta in a large bowl with egg, cream, milk, blue cheese and fennel; season. Transfer mixture to an oiled deep 2-litre (8-cup) ovenproof dish; sprinkle with parmesan.

5 Bake, uncovered, for 15 minutes or until pasta is heated through. Toss tomato in oil in a small bowl. Top pasta with tomato mixture; sprinkle with ¼ cup of the reserved fennel fronds before serving.

TEST KITCHEN NOTES

SWAP BLUE CHEESE FOR A MILDER CHEESE, IF YOU PREFER. RICOTTA, FETTA OR CREAM CHEESE WOULD ALL WORK WELL.

PORK, MUSHROOM AND SAGE LASAGNE

PREP + COOK TIME 2 HOURS ◆ SERVES 6

1 tablespoon olive oil

1 small brown onion (80g), chopped finely

2 cloves garlic, crushed

1 cured chorizo sausage (170g), chopped finely

315g (10 ounces) minced (ground) pork

315g (10 ounces) minced (ground) veal

½ cup (125ml) marsala

½ cup (125ml) chicken stock

6 large sheets dried lasagne (250g)

¾ cup (60g) finely grated parmesan

12 fresh sage leaves, torn

fresh sage leaves, extra, torn

MUSHROOM MIXTURE

20g (¾ ounce) dried porcini mushrooms

½ cup (125ml) boiling water

15g (½ ounce) butter

1 small brown onion (80g), chopped finely

1 clove garlic, crushed

185g (6 ounces) button mushrooms, sliced thinly

1 tablespoon coarsely shredded fresh sage

WHITE SAUCE

60g (2 ounces) butter

⅓ cup (50g) plain (all-purpose) flour

1.25 litres (5 cups) hot milk

1 Make mushroom mixture and white sauce.

2 Reserve a third of the white sauce; combine remaining sauce with mushroom mixture.

3 Preheat oven to 200°C/400°F.

4 Heat oil in a large frying pan over high heat; cook onion, garlic and chorizo, stirring, for 3 minutes or until onion softens. Add pork and veal to pan; cook, stirring, until browned. Add marsala, stock and reserved porcini mushroom liquid; bring to the boil. Reduce heat, simmer, uncovered, for 10 minutes or until liquid is reduced by about a third.

5 Oil a 2-litre (8-cup) ovenproof dish. Place two lasagne sheets in base of dish. Top with half the mince mixture, then half the mushroom mixture; sprinkle with ¼ cup of the parmesan. Repeat layering, finishing with remaining two pasta sheets. Spread with reserved white sauce; top with sage and remaining parmesan.

6 Bake lasagne, uncovered, for 40 minutes or until browned lightly. Stand 5 minutes before serving, topped with extra sage.

MUSHROOM MIXTURE Combine porcini mushrooms with the boiling water in a medium heatproof bowl; stand 5 minutes. Drain, reserve liquid (for mince mixture); chop porcini mushrooms finely. Heat butter in a large frying pan over medium heat, add onion and garlic; cook, stirring, for 4 minutes or until onion softens. Add porcini and button mushrooms; cook, stirring, until mushrooms are browned. Add sage; season to taste.

WHITE SAUCE Melt butter in a medium saucepan over high heat, add flour; cook, stirring, until mixture bubbles. Gradually stir in milk; cook, stirring, until mixture boils and thickens. Simmer, stirring, about 2 minutes; season to taste.

PORCINI MUSHROOMS

DRIED ITALIAN MUSHROOMS, ARE AVAILABLE FROM SOME LARGER SUPERMARKETS, GOURMET FOOD STORES AND DELICATESSENS. SOME BUTCHERS SELL A PORK AND VEAL MINCE MIXTURE, THIS IS FINE TO USE HERE – YOU WILL NEED TO BUY 630G (1¼ POUNDS).

PORK GREEN CURRY

PREP + COOK TIME 35 MINUTES ◆ SERVES 4

800g (1½ pounds) minced (ground) pork

3 teaspoons finely grated fresh ginger

1 fresh long red chilli, chopped finely

2 cloves garlic, crushed

⅓ cup coarsely chopped fresh coriander (cilantro)

1 tablespoon peanut oil

¼ cup (75g) green curry paste

2 x 400ml canned coconut milk

⅔ cup (130g) jasmine rice

2 tablespoons lime juice

1 tablespoon fish sauce

1 tablespoon grated palm sugar

200g (6½ ounces) snake beans, cut into 5cm (2-inch) lengths

⅓ cup loosely packed fresh thai basil leaves

1 Combine pork, ginger, chilli, garlic and half the coriander in a medium bowl; roll level tablespoons of the mixture into balls. Heat oil in a large frying pan over high heat; cook meatballs, in batches, for 5 minutes or until browned all over. Remove from pan.

2 Cook paste in same pan over medium heat, stirring, for 30 seconds or until fragrant. Add coconut milk; bring to the boil. Reduce heat; simmer, stirring occasionally, about 10 minutes.

3 Boil, steam or microwave rice until tender.

4 Return meatballs to pan with juice, sauce, sugar and beans; simmer, covered, for 5 minutes or until meatballs are cooked through. Remove from heat; stir in basil and remaining coriander. Serve curry with rice.

APRICOT CHICKEN WITH CREAMY RICE

PREP + COOK TIME 1 HOUR ◆ SERVES 4

2 tablespoons vegetable oil

12 chicken lovely legs (1.2kg)

2 large brown onions (400g), sliced thickly

2 teaspoons finely grated fresh ginger

2 cloves garlic, crushed

3 trimmed celery stalks (300g), chopped finely

425g (13½ ounces) canned apricot nectar

1 cup (250ml) water

40g (1½ ounces) packaged french onion soup mix

1 cup (200g) calrose rice

30g (1 ounce) baby spinach

1 tablespoon finely chopped fresh flat-leaf parsley

1 Heat half the oil in a large frying pan over high heat. Cook chicken, in batches, until browned all over; drain on paper towel.

2 Heat remaining oil in the same pan; cook onion, ginger, garlic and celery, stirring, for 10 minutes or until onion and celery are browned lightly.

3 Return chicken to pan with nectar, the water and soup mix; bring to the boil. Simmer, covered, about 10 minutes. Add rice; simmer, uncovered, stirring occasionally, for 30 minutes or until rice is tender. Stir in spinach. Sprinkle with parsley to serve.

TEST KITCHEN NOTES

WE USED TRIMMED, SKINLESS CHICKEN DRUMSTICKS, KNOWN AS 'LOVELY LEGS' FOR THIS RECIPE; THEY WILL SAVE YOU TIME BY NOT HAVING TO REMOVE THE SKIN.

SERVING
SUGGESTION
STEAMED
VEGETABLES
OR A SALAD.

KUMARA AND COCONUT CURRY

PREP + COOK TIME 30 MINUTES ◆ SERVES 4

¼ cup (60ml) olive oil

1 medium leek (350g), white part only, sliced thinly

2 cloves garlic, crushed

⅓ cup (100g) korma paste

300g (9½ ounces) kumara (orange sweet potato), chopped coarsely

270ml canned coconut milk

1 cup (250ml) vegetable stock

400g (12½ ounces) canned diced tomatoes

800g (1½ pounds) canned chickpeas (garbanzo beans), rinsed, drained

400g (12½ ounces) cauliflower, cut into florets

1 tablespoon black mustard seeds

12 fresh curry leaves

200g (6½ ounces) cavolo nero (tuscan cabbage), lightly washed, chopped coarsely

1 Heat 1 tablespoon of the oil in a large saucepan over medium-high heat; cook leek and garlic, stirring, for 2 minutes or until softened.

2 Add paste to pan; cook, stirring, about 2 minutes. Add kumara, coconut milk, stock, tomatoes and chickpeas; bring to the boil. Reduce heat; simmer, covered, for 6 minutes or until kumara is almost tender. Stir in cauliflower, cook for 5 minutes or until tender.

3 Meanwhile, heat remaining oil in a large frying pan over medium heat; cook seeds, stirring, for 1 minute or until seeds pop. Add curry leaves; cook about 1 minute, then stir in cavolo nero. Cook, covered, until cavolo nero is just wilted. Season to taste.

4 Stir cavolo nero into curry mixture to serve.

TEST KITCHEN NOTES

SWAP BROCCOLI FOR CAULIFLOWER AND KALE OR SPINACH FOR CAVOLO NERO. COOK CAVOLO NERO WITH WATER STILL CLINGING TO IT. USE CORIANDER IF CURRY LEAVES ARE UNAVAILABLE.

OVEN-BAKED RISOTTO WITH CHICKEN, ROCKET AND SEMI-DRIED TOMATO

PREP + COOK TIME 45 MINUTES ◆ SERVES 4

1 tablespoon olive oil

1 large brown onion (200g), sliced thinly

2 cloves garlic, crushed

2 cups (400g) arborio rice

¾ cup (180ml) dry white wine

1 litre (4 cups) chicken stock

4 chicken breast fillets (680g)

100g (3 ounces) baby rocket leaves (arugula)

250g (8 ounces) heirloom cherry tomatoes, halved

½ cup (40g) finely grated parmesan

1 tablespoon coarsely chopped fresh flat-leaf parsley

1   Preheat oven to 180°C/350°F.

2   Heat oil in a shallow 3-litre (12-cup) flameproof baking dish over medium-high heat; cook onion and garlic, stirring, for 4 minutes or until onion softens. Add rice; stir to coat in onion mixture. Stir in wine and stock; bring to the boil.

3   Place chicken, in a single layer, on top of the rice mixture; cover. Transfer to oven; bake for 25 minutes or until rice is tender and chicken is cooked through. Remove chicken from pan; stand 5 minutes.

4   Stir rocket, tomato and a third of the parmesan into risotto. Serve risotto with chicken; sprinkle remaining parmesan and parsley over chicken, season to taste.

TEST KITCHEN NOTES

WE USED A SEMILLON-STYLE WINE, BUT YOU CAN USE YOUR FAVOURITE DRY WHITE WINE. THIS RECIPE IS BEST MADE CLOSE TO SERVING.

SERVING
SUGGESTION
STEAMED GREEN
BEANS OR
ASPARAGUS.

CHICKEN KIEV

PREP + COOK TIME 45 MINUTES (+ REFRIGERATION) ◆ SERVES 4

100g (3 ounces) butter, softened

3 cloves garlic, crushed

1 teaspoon finely grated lemon rind

2 tablespoons each finely chopped fresh flat-leaf parsley and chives

4 chicken breast fillets (800g)

⅓ cup (50g) plain (all-purpose) flour

2 eggs, beaten lightly

2 cups (140g) panko (japanese) breadcrumbs

vegetable oil, for deep-frying

600g (1¼-pound) tub mashed potato

340g (11 ounces) asparagus, trimmed

lemon wedges, to serve

1 Combine butter, garlic, rind, parsley and chives in a small bowl; beat with a wooden spoon until combined. Spoon mixture onto a piece of plastic wrap, shape into a 20cm (8-inch) log; wrap tightly, freeze until firm.

2 Cut chicken in half horizontally almost all the way through. Open out fillets, place between sheets of plastic wrap and gently pound with a meat mallet until 1cm (½-inch) thick.

3 Cut butter log into 4 pieces; place a piece of butter at one end of a fillet. Roll once, fold in sides, roll up. Toss chicken roll in flour; dip in egg, then roll in breadcrumbs. Repeat to make a total of 4 rolls. Refrigerate 30 minutes.

4 Heat oil in a medium saucepan to 160°C/325°F (or until a cube of bread turns golden in 30 seconds). Deep-fry chicken, in two batches, for 10 minutes or until golden and cooked through. Drain well on paper towel.

5 Meanwhile, microwave mashed potato according to directions on tub. Boil, steam or microwave asparagus until tender. Serve chicken with vegetables and lemon.

TEST KITCHEN NOTES

THIS RECIPE CAN ALSO BE MADE INTO CHICKEN CORDON BLEU; AFTER THE FILLETS HAVE BEEN CUT IN HALF, PLACE A PIECE OF SWISS CHEESE AND SMOKED HAM INTO THE OPENING, SECURE CLOSED WITH TOOTHPICKS. CONTINUE CRUMBING CHICKEN FILLETS BEFORE SHALLOW-FRYING.

LENTIL COTTAGE PIE

PREP + COOK TIME 55 MINUTES (+ STANDING) ◆ SERVES 4

800g (1½ pounds) medium potatoes, quartered

2 tablespoons butter

1 medium brown onion (150g), chopped finely

1 clove garlic, crushed

400g (12½ ounces) canned crushed tomatoes

1 cup (250ml) vegetable stock

1 cup (250ml) water

2 tablespoons tomato paste

⅓ cup (80ml) dry red wine

⅔ cup (130g) red lentils

1 medium carrot (120g), chopped finely

½ cup (60g) frozen peas, thawed

2 tablespoons worcestershire sauce

⅓ cup coarsely chopped fresh flat-leaf parsley

1 Preheat oven to 220°C/425°F.

2 Boil, steam or microwave potato until tender; drain. Mash in a large bowl with half the butter.

3 Melt remaining butter in a deep medium frying pan over medium heat; cook onion and garlic, stirring, for 4 minutes or until onion softens. Add tomatoes, stock, the water, paste, wine, lentils and carrot to pan; bring to the boil.

4 Reduce heat; simmer, uncovered, about 15 minutes, stirring occasionally. Add peas, sauce and parsley; cook, uncovered, about 5 minutes.

5 Spoon lentil mixture into a shallow 1-litre (4-cup) ovenproof dish. Spread mashed potato on top. Bake, uncovered, about 20 minutes. Stand pie 10 minutes before serving.

TEST KITCHEN NOTES

WE USED A PINOT NOIR-STYLE WINE.
STIR 1 CUP FINELY GRATED PARMESAN
INTO MASHED POTATO BEFORE BAKING PIE.

SERVING
SUGGESTION
GREEN LEAFY
SALAD.

WILD MUSHROOM RISOTTO

PREP + COOK TIME 40 MINUTES ◆ SERVES 4

15g (½ ounce) dried porcini mushrooms

1 litre (4 cups) vegetable stock

2 cups (500ml) water

50g (1½ ounces) butter

100g (3 ounces) chestnut mushrooms, trimmed

100g (3 ounces) button mushrooms, sliced thickly

2 flat mushrooms (160g), halved, sliced thickly

4 shallots (100g), chopped finely

2 cloves garlic, crushed

2 cups (400g) arborio rice

½ cup (125ml) dry white wine

½ cup (40g) finely grated parmesan

2 tablespoons finely chopped fresh parsley

1 Combine porcini mushrooms, stock and the water in a medium saucepan; bring to the boil. Reduce heat; simmer, covered.

2 Meanwhile, melt 30g of the butter in a large saucepan over medium-high heat; add remaining mushrooms to pan. Cook, stirring, for 5 minutes or until mushrooms are tender and liquid evaporates; remove from pan.

3 Melt remaining butter in same pan; cook shallots and garlic, stirring, for 3 minutes or until shallots soften. Add rice; stir to coat rice in butter mixture. Return mushrooms to pan with wine; bring to the boil. Reduce heat; simmer, uncovered, until liquid has almost evaporated.

4 Add 1 cup of the simmering stock mixture to pan; cook, stirring, over low heat, until stock is absorbed. Continue adding stock mixture, in 1-cup batches, stirring, until absorbed between additions. Total cooking time should be 25 minutes or until rice is tender.

5 Sprinkle risotto with parmesan and parsley to serve. Accompany with crusty bread, if you like.

TEST KITCHEN NOTES

DRIED MUSHROOMS ARE AVAILABLE FROM DELIS AND SOME LARGER SUPERMARKETS. WE USED A CHARDONNAY-STYLE WINE.

RAVIOLI WITH PUMPKIN AND SAGE SAUCE

PREP + COOK TIME 35 MINUTES ◆ SERVES 4

1 tablespoon olive oil

8 large fresh sage leaves

500g (1 pound) pumpkin, cut into 1cm (½-inch) cubes

4 green onions (scallions), chopped coarsely

1 tablespoon thinly shredded fresh sage

1 tablespoon white balsamic vinegar

625g (1¼ pounds) fresh spinach and ricotta ravioli

100g (3 ounces) butter

¾ cup (180ml) vegetable stock

¼ cup (40g) pine nuts

1 Heat oil in a large frying pan over high heat; cook sage leaves, stirring gently, until bright green and crisp. Drain on paper towel.

2 Cook pumpkin in same pan, uncovered, stirring occasionally, for 15 minutes or until browned lightly and just tender. Add onion, shredded sage and vinegar; cook, stirring, about 1 minute. Remove from pan; cover to keep warm.

3 Meanwhile, cook ravioli in a large saucepan of boiling water until just tender; drain. Cover to keep warm.

4 Place butter in same cleaned pan; bring to the boil. Reduce heat; simmer, uncovered, for 5 minutes or until nut-brown in colour. Add stock to pan; bring to the boil then reduce heat to low. Return pumpkin mixture to pan with ravioli; stir over low heat until sauce is heated through, season to taste. Top with sage leaves and sprinkle with pine nuts.

TEST KITCHEN NOTES

RAVIOLI, SMALL SQUARE PASTA POCKETS STUFFED WITH MEAT, CHEESE OR VEGETABLES, IS SOLD IN THE REFRIGERATED SECTION AT SUPERMARKETS.

SERVING
SUGGESTION
CRUSTY BREAD.

GARLIC AND CHILLI MUSSELS

PREP + COOK TIME 20 MINUTES ◆ SERVES 4

60g (2 ounces) butter, chopped

3 cloves garlic, chopped finely

1 fresh long red chilli, sliced thinly

⅓ cup (80ml) dry white wine

1kg (2 pounds) small black mussels, scrubbed, bearded

⅓ cup coarsely chopped fresh flat-leaf parsley

1 Heat butter, garlic and chilli in a large saucepan, stirring, until fragrant.

2 Add wine to pan; bring to the boil. Add mussels; cover with a tight-fitting lid. Cook for 5 minutes, shaking pan occasionally, or until mussels open. Stir in parsley; season to taste.

TEST KITCHEN NOTES

BUY PRE-CLEANED, BEARDED MUSSELS. IT'S A MYTH THAT UNOPENED MUSSELS SHOULD BE DISCARDED. IF YOU CAN PRY THEM OPEN, THEY ARE SAFE TO EAT. THE REASON THEY DON'T OPEN IS SIMPLY DUE TO HOW THE SHELL HAS FORMED.

FETTUCCINE BOLOGNESE

PREP + COOK TIME 30 MINUTES ◆ SERVES 4

2 teaspoons olive oil

1 medium brown onion (150g), chopped finely

2 cloves garlic, crushed

1 medium carrot (120g), chopped finely

1 trimmed celery stalk (100g), chopped finely

500g (1 pound) minced (ground) beef

2 cups (500ml) passata

½ cup (125ml) beef stock

375g (12 ounces) fettuccine

1 Heat oil in a large frying pan over high heat; cook onion and garlic, stirring, for 3 minutes or until onion softens. Add carrot and celery to pan; cook, stirring, for 5 minutes or until vegetables are just tender.

2 Add beef; cook, stirring, until beef is changed in colour. Add passata and stock; bring to the boil. Reduce heat; simmer, uncovered, for 15 minutes or until the mixture thickens slightly. Season to taste.

3 Meanwhile, cook pasta in a large saucepan of boiling water until just tender; drain.

4 Serve pasta topped with bolognese sauce.

TEST KITCHEN NOTES

PASSATA IS SIEVED TOMATO PUREE AVAILABLE FROM SUPERMARKETS. THE FLAVOUR OF THE BOLOGNESE WILL IMPROVE IF IT IS MADE A DAY AHEAD; REHEAT JUST BEFORE SERVING. BOLOGNESE IS SUITABLE TO FREEZE; THAW OVERNIGHT IN THE FRIDGE BEFORE REHEATING.

SERVING SUGGESTION
GREEN LEAFY
SALAD AND A
LOAF OF CRUSTY
CIABATTA BREAD.

SERVING SUGGESTION
GREEN LEAF AND MIXED HERB SALAD

CAULIFLOWER AND CHEESE PASTA BAKE

PREP + COOK TIME 25 MINUTES ◆ SERVES 4

250g (8 ounces) spiral pasta

30g (1 ounce) butter

2 tablespoons plain (all-purpose) flour

2 cups (500ml) milk

1½ cups (150g) coarsely grated mozzarella

2 tablespoons coarsely chopped fresh flat-leaf parsley

500g (1 pound) frozen cauliflower florets, thawed

1 egg, beaten lightly

¼ cup (20g) panko (japanese) breadcrumbs

½ teaspoon ground nutmeg

1 Preheat grill (broiler). Oil a 2-litre (8-cup) ovenproof dish.

2 Cook pasta in a large saucepan of boiling water until almost tender; drain.

3 Meanwhile, to make cheese sauce, melt butter in a medium saucepan over medium heat, add flour; cook, stirring, until bubbling. Gradually stir in milk; cook, stirring, until mixture boils and thickens. Remove from heat; stir in 1 cup of the mozzarella, and parsley.

4 Combine pasta, cheese sauce and cauliflower in a large bowl; stir in egg. Spoon mixture into dish, top with combined breadcrumbs and remaining mozzarella; sprinkle with nutmeg.

5 Place dish under hot grill for 10 minutes or until top is golden.

PEPPERED STEAK SANDWICH WITH GRILLED TOMATOES

PREP + COOK TIME 20 MINUTES ◆ SERVES 4

2 tablespoons olive oil

2 teaspoons cracked black pepper

4 beef minute steaks (400g)

250g (8 ounces) cherry truss tomatoes, cut into four clusters

8 slices sourdough bread (560g)

⅓ cup (100g) aïoli

½ cup (70g) caramelised onion relish

½ cup loosely packed trimmed watercress

1 Combine oil and pepper in a shallow dish; add steaks, turn to coat.

2 Heat an oiled chargrill pan (or barbecue or grill) over medium-high heat; cook steaks for 2 minutes each side or until cooked as desired. Remove from pan, cover; rest 5 minutes.

3 Cook tomato clusters in same pan for 3 minutes or until softened. Remove from pan.

4 Toast bread slices in same pan about 30 seconds each side. Spread aïoli onto half the toasted slices; top each with steak, relish and watercress, then remaining toasted slices. Serve sandwiches with tomato clusters.

TEST KITCHEN NOTES

AÏOLI IS GARLIC MAYONNAISE, AVAILABLE FROM THE CONDIMENT AISLE IN MOST SUPERMARKETS.

CHORIZO AND TOMATO PASTA

PREP + COOK TIME 15 MINUTES ◆ SERVES 4

375g (12 ounces) penne pasta

2 chorizo sausages (340g), sliced thinly

2 cups (560g) bottled tomato pasta sauce

100g (3 ounces) baby spinach leaves

1 Cook pasta in a large saucepan of boiling water until tender; drain.

2 Meanwhile, cook chorizo in a heated oiled large frying pan over high heat for 3 minutes or until browned.

3 Add sauce; bring to the boil. Reduce heat, simmer, uncovered, for 5 minutes or until sauce thickens.

4 Add spinach and pasta to pan; stir gently until mixture is heated through. Sprinkle with grated parmesan, if you like.

COMFORT

1

HOT-SMOKED SALMON AND DILL

PREP + COOK TIME 1 HOUR ♦ SERVES 2

Boil 3½ cups chicken stock, ½ cup dry white wine and ¼ teaspoon saffron in a medium saucepan, then simmer, covered. Heat 25g (¾ ounce) butter in a large saucepan over medium heat; cook 1 large finely chopped onion until soft. Stir 1¾ cups arborio rice into the onion mixture. Add 1 cup of the stock mixture, stirring over low heat until liquid is absorbed. Continue adding stock mixture in 1-cup batches, stirring after each addition until liquid is absorbed. Total cooking time should be 35 minutes or until rice is tender. Stir in 25g (¾ ounce) extra butter, 100g (3 ounces) flaked hot-smoked salmon and 2 tablespoons finely grated parmesan; sprinkle with 2 tablespoons chopped fresh dill to serve.

2

PUMPKIN AND SPINACH

PREP + COOK TIME 1 HOUR ♦ SERVES 2

Boil, steam or microwave 100g (3 ounces) chopped pumpkin. Meanwhile, boil 3½ cups chicken stock, ½ cup dry white wine and ¼ teaspoon saffron in a medium saucepan, then simmer, covered. Heat 25g (¾ ounce) butter in a large saucepan over medium heat; cook 1 large finely chopped onion until soft. Stir 1¾ cups arborio rice into the onion mixture. Add 1 cup of the stock mixture, stirring over low heat until liquid is absorbed. Continue adding stock mixture in 1-cup batches, stirring after each addition until liquid is absorbed. Total cooking time should be 35 minutes or until rice is tender. Stir in 25g (¾ ounce) extra butter, pumpkin, 50g (1½ ounce) baby spinach leaves and 2 tablespoons finely grated parmesan until hot. Sprinkle with 2 tablespoons fresh baby basil leaves to serve.

RISOTTO

3

RISOTTO MILANESE

PREP + COOK TIME 1 HOUR ♦ SERVES 2

Boil 3½ cups chicken stock, ½ cup dry white wine and ¼ teaspoon saffron in a medium saucepan, then simmer, covered. Heat 25g (¾ ounce) butter in a large saucepan over medium heat; cook 1 large finely chopped onion until soft. Stir 1¾ cups arborio rice into the onion mixture. Add 1 cup of the stock mixture, stirring over low heat until liquid is absorbed. Continue adding stock mixture in 1-cup batches, stirring after each addition until liquid is absorbed. Total cooking time should be 35 minutes or until rice is tender. Stir in 25g (¾ ounce) extra butter and 2 tablespoons each finely grated parmesan and chopped fresh parsley.

4

PROSCIUTTO AND PEAS

PREP + COOK TIME 1 HOUR ♦ SERVES 2

Boil 3½ cups chicken stock, ½ cup dry white wine and ¼ teaspoon saffron in a medium saucepan, then simmer, covered. Heat 25g (¾ ounce) butter in a large saucepan over medium heat; cook 1 large finely chopped onion until soft. Stir 1¾ cups arborio rice into the onion mixture. Add 1 cup of the stock mixture, stirring over low heat until liquid is absorbed. Continue adding stock mixture in 1-cup batches, stirring after each addition until liquid is absorbed. Total cooking time should be 35 minutes or until rice is tender. Stir in 25g (¾ ounce) extra butter, 4 slices roughly chopped prosciutto, ½ cup thawed frozen peas and 2 tablespoons finely grated parmesan, stirring until peas are hot. Sprinkle with 2 tablespoons fresh chervil to serve.

1

POTATO MASH

PREP + COOK TIME 30 MINUTES ◆ SERVES 4

Place 1kg (2 pounds) coarsely chopped peeled lasoda potatoes in a medium saucepan with enough cold water to barely cover potato. Boil, uncovered, over medium heat, for 15 minutes or until potato is tender; drain. Using the back of a wooden spoon, push potato through a fine sieve into a large bowl. Stir 40g (1½ ounces) butter and ¾ cup hot milk into potato, folding gently until mash is smooth and fluffy.

2

PEA MASH

PREP + COOK TIME 30 MINUTES ◆ SERVES 4

Place 1kg (2 pounds) coarsely chopped peeled pontiac potatoes in a medium saucepan with enough cold water to barely cover potato. Boil, uncovered, over medium heat, for 15 minutes or until potato is almost tender. Add 1½ cups frozen peas to potato; boil, uncovered, for 3 minutes or until tender; drain. Mash potato mixture with 50g (1½ ounces) butter and ¾ cup hot milk; stir in peas.

3

PUMPKIN MASH

PREP + COOK TIME 30 MINUTES ◆ SERVES 4

Boil, steam or microwave 500g (1 pound) coarsely chopped peeled pontiac potatoes and 500g (1 pound) coarsely chopped peeled pumpkin together until tender; drain. Mash potato and pumpkin; stir in 30g (1 ounce) butter. Season to taste.

4

KUMARA MASH

PREP + COOK TIME 30 MINUTES ◆ SERVES 4

Boil, steam or microwave 500g (1 pound) coarsely chopped peeled kumara and 500g (1 pound) coarsely chopped peeled potatoes together until tender; drain. Mash in a large heatproof bowl. Combine ¼ cup chicken stock and 40g (1½ ounces) butter in a small saucepan over medium-high heat until butter is melted. Stir into kumara mixture until combined. Season to taste.

SWEET

AT THE END OF THE FAMILY
TABLE ARE THE SWEETS
EVERYONE'S BEEN WAITING
FOR SO PATIENTLY. WITH
THE HELP OF THESE RECIPES
YOU CAN ALL INDULGE
IN AN ARRAY OF RICH
FLAVOURS AFTER DINNER.

APPLE AND RASPBERRY CRUMBLES

PREP + COOK TIME 35 MINUTES ◆ SERVES 4

4 medium apples (600g), peeled, chopped coarsely

2 teaspoons finely grated lemon rind

¼ cup (60ml) lemon juice

¼ cup (55g) firmly packed brown sugar

2 teaspoons mixed spice

2 tablespoons water

500g (1 pound) raspberries

125g (4 ounces) scotch finger biscuits

20g (¾ ounce) butter

20g (¾ ounce) natural almond flakes

1 Preheat oven to 220°C/425°F.

2 Cook apple, rind, juice and sugar in a large frying pan until apple begins to caramelise. Stir in mixed spice, the water and raspberries. Spoon mixture into four 1-cup (250ml) shallow ovenproof dishes.

3 Crumble biscuits into a small bowl. Rub in butter until mixture clumps slightly; stir in almonds. Sprinkle crumb mixture on fruit. Place dishes on an oven tray.

4 Bake for 10 minutes or until crumbles are heated through.

TEST KITCHEN NOTES

USE GRANNY SMITH APPLES FOR A SLIGHTLY TART FLAVOUR. RASPBERRIES CAN BE EITHER FRESH OR FROZEN.

CHOCOLATE AND CARAMEL PUDDINGS

PREP + COOK TIME 30 MINUTES ♦ MAKES 4

125g (4 ounces) butter, softened

⅔ cup (150g) firmly packed brown sugar

2 eggs

½ cup (75g) plain (all-purpose) flour

¼ cup (25g) cocoa powder

1½ tablespoons milk

12 caramel-filled chocolate squares (75g)

1 Preheat oven to 200°C/400°F. Grease four 1-cup (250ml) ovenproof dishes.

2 Beat butter and sugar in a small bowl with an electric mixer until light and fluffy. Beat in eggs, one at a time. Stir in sifted flour, cocoa and milk.

3 Divide two-thirds of the mixture into dishes; place three caramel chocolate squares in centre of each dish. Spoon remaining mixture over chocolates; smooth surface.

4 Bake for 20 minutes or until tops are firm to the touch. Serve immediately.

SERVING
SUGGESTION
POURING CREAM
OR ICE-CREAM
DUSTED WITH SIFTED
COCOA POWDER

SMOOTH RICOTTA IS SOLD IN TUBS AND IS MUCH WETTER THAN THE FIRM RICOTTA CUT FROM A WHEEL. IF YOU USE FIRM RICOTTA, YOU WILL NEED TO INCREASE THE AMOUNT OF BUTTERMILK BY ¼ CUP.

BLUEBERRY RICOTTA PIKELETS WITH CARAMELISED ORANGES

PREP + COOK TIME 30 MINUTES ◆ SERVES 6

2 cups (300g) self-raising flour

¼ cup (55g) caster (superfine) sugar

2 eggs

1 cup (240g) smooth ricotta

1¼ cup (310ml) buttermilk

2 teaspoons finely grated orange rind

125g (4 ounces) fresh blueberries

cooking-oil spray

CARAMELISED ORANGES

4 medium oranges (960g)

¾ cup (165g) caster (superfine) sugar

¾ cup (180ml) water

¾ cup (180ml) orange juice

1 Process flour, sugar, eggs, ricotta, buttermilk and rind until combined. Transfer batter to a large jug; stir in berries.

2 Spray a heated large heavy-based frying pan with cooking oil. Pour 1 tablespoon of the batter for each pikelet into pan. Cook pikelets over medium heat until bubbles appear on surface; turn, brown other side. Remove from pan; cover to keep warm. Repeat with remaining batter.

3 Make caramelised oranges.

4 Serve pikelets with caramelised oranges.

CARAMELISED ORANGES Segment oranges over a small bowl. Stir sugar and the water in a medium saucepan over low heat, without boiling, until sugar dissolves. Bring to the boil; boil for 10 minutes or until caramel forms. Remove from heat, carefully stir in juice (take care as caramel will splatter); stir over heat until caramel pieces are dissolved. Stir in orange segments.

TEST KITCHEN NOTES

TO SEGMENT ORANGES, CUT OFF THE RIND WITH THE WHITE PITH, FOLLOWING THE CURVE OF THE FRUIT. CUT DOWN EITHER SIDE OF EACH SEGMENT CLOSE TO THE MEMBRANE TO RELEASE THE SEGMENT.

DARK CHOCOLATE AND RICOTTA MOUSSE

PREP + COOK TIME 20 MINUTES ◆ SERVES 6

⅓ cup (110g) rice malt syrup

1 tablespoon dutch-processed cocoa

2 tablespoons water

½ teaspoon vanilla extract

200g (6½ ounces) dark chocolate (70% cocoa), chopped coarsely

8 fresh dates (160g), pitted

½ cup (125ml) milk

2 cups (480g) soft ricotta

2 tablespoons pomegranate seeds

2 tablespoons chopped pistachios

1 Stir syrup, cocoa, the water and extract in a small saucepan over medium heat; bring to the boil. Remove from heat; cool.

2 Place chocolate in a small heatproof bowl over a small saucepan of simmering water (don't let the water touch the base of the bowl); stir until melted and smooth.

3 Process dates and milk until dates are finely chopped. Add ricotta; process until smooth. Add melted chocolate; process until well combined.

4 Spoon mousse into six ¾-cup (180ml) serving glasses. Spoon cocoa syrup on mousse; top with seeds and pistachios.

TEST KITCHEN NOTES

UNLIKE MOST MOUSSE RECIPES THIS CAN BE SERVED IMMEDIATELY. IF YOU WISH TO MAKE IT A DAY AHEAD, REFRIGERATE, COVERED, THEN BRING TO ROOM TEMPERATURE BEFORE SERVING.

POMEGRANATE SEEDS
CUT A WHOLE POMEGRANATE IN HALF CROSSWAYS; HOLD IT, CUT-SIDE DOWN, IN THE PALM OF YOUR HAND OVER A BOWL, HIT THE OUTSIDE FIRMLY WITH A WOODEN SPOON. THE SEEDS SHOULD FALL OUT EASILY; DISCARD ANY WHITE PITH THAT FALLS OUT WITH THEM.

PERSIMMONS
THERE ARE TWO TYPES OF PERSIMMON AVAILABLE IN AUTUMN: ASTRINGENT AND NON-ASTRINGENT. THE FIRST IS HEART-SHAPED AND EATEN VERY RIPE. THE OTHER, WHICH IS SOMETIMES SOLD AS FUJI FRUIT, IS SQUAT AND EATEN CRISP. USE EITHER VARIETY FOR THIS RECIPE.

HONEY AND LIME BAKED PERSIMMONS

PREP + COOK TIME 25 MINUTES ◆ SERVES 4

4 persimmons (1kg), each cut into 6 wedges

1 lime, sliced thinly

20g (¾ ounce) fresh ginger, sliced thinly

1½ tablespoons honey

200g (6½ ounces) passionfruit frozen yoghurt

1 tablespoon lime rind strips

1 Preheat oven to 200°C/400°F. Cut four 35cm (14-inch) pieces of baking paper.

2 Place pieces of paper lengthways in front of you then divide persimmon wedges among baking paper, placing them crossways in the centre. Top with lime slices and ginger; drizzle with honey. Bring short edges of paper together, fold over several times to secure, then tuck sides under to form a parcel. Place parcels on two oven trays.

3 Bake for 15 minutes or until persimmon is soft. Serve opened parcels topped with spoonfuls of frozen yoghurt and lime rind.

TEST KITCHEN NOTES

USE A ZESTER TO MAKE THE LIME RIND STRIPS. IF YOU DON'T HAVE ONE, FINELY GRATE THE RIND INSTEAD.

LEMON CURD MERINGUE CAKE

**PREP + COOK TIME 1 HOUR 45 MINUTES
(+ REFRIGERATION, COOLING & STANDING) ◆ SERVES 12**

1 cup (150g) almonds

4 egg whites

1 cup (220g) caster (superfine) sugar

125g (4 ounces) white chocolate, grated coarsely

600ml thick (double) cream

125g (4 ounces) fresh blueberries

LEMON CURD

250g (8 ounces) cold butter, chopped coarsely

2 eggs, beaten lightly

2 egg yolks

⅔ cup (160ml) lemon juice

1⅓ cups (300g) caster (superfine) sugar

1 Make lemon curd.

2 Preheat oven to 160°C/325°F. Insert the base of a 24cm (9½-inch) springform pan upside down to make it easier to remove the cake. Grease and line base with baking paper.

3 Spread almonds, in a single layer, on an oven tray; roast, uncovered, for 12 minutes or until skins begin to split. Cool. Chop almonds finely.

4 Beat egg whites and ¼ cup of the sugar in a small bowl with an electric mixer until firm peaks form. Add remaining sugar; beat on high speed for 5 minutes or until sugar is dissolved. Fold in chocolate and almonds. Spread mixture into pan.

5 Bake about 40 minutes. Cool in pan.

6 Whisk cream in a small bowl with a wire whisk until soft peaks form; fold half the cream into lemon curd. Using a spoon, gently push down on meringue. Spoon curd mixture onto meringue. Refrigerate 1 hour until firm.

7 Just before serving, spoon remaining whipped cream onto cake; top with blueberries.

LEMON CURD Place butter in a medium saucepan; strain beaten egg into pan. Add remaining ingredients; stir over low heat, without boiling, for 10 minutes or until mixture thickly coats the back of a spoon. Transfer curd to a medium heatproof bowl; refrigerate until cold.

BERRY HAZELNUT CUPS

PREP TIME 25 MINUTES ◆ SERVES 6

250g (8 ounces) raspberries

2 tablespoons icing (confectioners') sugar

300ml thickened (heavy) cream

2 tablespoons hazelnut-flavoured liqueur

6 brandy baskets (90g)

⅓ cup (45g) coarsely chopped roasted peeled hazelnuts

1 Blend or process half the raspberries and half the sugar until smooth; strain through a fine sieve into a small jug.

2 Beat cream, liqueur and remaining sugar in a small bowl with an electric mixer until soft peaks form.

3 Spoon cream into brandy baskets; top with remaining raspberries and hazelnuts. Drizzle with raspberry sauce.

TEST KITCHEN NOTES

WE USED FRANGELICO IN THIS RECIPE BUT YOU CAN USE YOUR FAVOURITE HAZELNUT-FLAVOURED LIQUEUR.

CHAMPAGNE AND ORANGE FRENCH MACAROON TRIFLE

PREP + COOK TIME 1 HOUR (+ REFRIGERATION) ◆ SERVES 10

7 vanilla french macaroons (112g)

7 blood orange french macaroons (112g)

2 tablespoons natural sliced almonds, toasted lightly

CHAMPAGNE AND ORANGE JELLY

6 teaspoons gelatine

2 cups (500ml) fresh orange juice, strained

1 cup (250ml) champagne or sparkling wine

½ cup (110g) caster (superfine) sugar

2 medium oranges (480g)

CANDIED ORANGE RIND

2 medium oranges (480g)

1 cup (250ml) water

½ cup (110g) caster (superfine) sugar

ORANGE-SCENTED CUSTARD

1½ cups (375ml) thick custard

1½ cups (375g) mascarpone cheese

2 tablespoons finely grated orange rind

1 tablespoon orange-flavoured liqueur

VANILLA CREAM

1 vanilla bean, split lengthways

2 cups (500ml) thickened (heavy) cream

¼ cup (40g) icing (confectioners') sugar

1 Make champagne and orange jelly. Pour into a 3-litre (12-cup) deep glass dish. Cover; refrigerate 3 hours or until set.

2 Make candied orange rind, orange-scented custard and vanilla cream.

3 Just before serving, top jelly with macaroons, custard and cream. Top with almonds, candied rind and any syrup from the rind.

CHAMPAGNE AND ORANGE JELLY Stir gelatine into ½ cup of the juice in a small bowl until combined. Stand 5 minutes. Place remaining juice, champagne and sugar in a medium saucepan over medium heat; stir until sugar is dissolved. Bring to the boil; boil about 1 minute. Remove from heat; stir in gelatine mixture until gelatine is dissolved. Segment oranges; add segments to juice mixture.

CANDIED ORANGE RIND Remove rind from oranges with a zester. Place the water in a small saucepan; bring to the boil. Add rind; simmer about 1 minute. Drain rind; reserve ½ cup of the liquid. Place reserved liquid and sugar in same pan over medium heat; stir until sugar is dissolved. Bring to the boil; simmer, uncovered, about 1 minute. Add rind; simmer, uncovered, for 5 minutes or until candied. Drain. Spread out on a sheet of baking paper to cool.

ORANGE-SCENTED CUSTARD Whisk ingredients together in a large bowl.

VANILLA CREAM Scrape seeds from vanilla bean. Beat cream, seeds and sugar in a medium bowl with an electric mixer until soft peaks form.

HONEY NOUGAT AND ESPRESSO SEMIFREDDO

PREP TIME 30 MINUTES (+ FREEZING) ◆ SERVES 8

3 eggs, separated

1 teaspoon vanilla extract

1 tablespoon honey

½ cup (80g) icing (confectioners') sugar

⅔ cup (160ml) pouring cream

80g (2½ ounces) honey and nut nougat, chopped finely

140g (4½ ounces) chocolate-coated honeycomb, chopped coarsely

ESPRESSO LAYER

3 eggs, separated

1 teaspoon vanilla extract

2 tablespoons instant coffee granules

½ cup (80g) icing (confectioners') sugar

⅔ cup (160ml) pouring cream

1 Grease an 8cm x 11cm x 26cm (3¼-inch x 4½-inch x 10½-inch) loaf pan; line base and sides with baking paper, extending paper 5cm (2 inches) over long sides.

2 Beat egg yolks, extract, honey and 2 tablespoons of the sifted sugar in a small bowl with an electric mixer until thick and pale. Transfer mixture to a large bowl.

3 Beat egg whites in a clean small bowl with electric mixer until soft peaks form. Gradually add remaining sugar; beat until thick and glossy.

4 Beat cream in another clean small bowl with electric mixer until soft peaks form.

5 Fold egg whites, cream and nougat into egg yolk mixture. Pour mixture into pan. Cover; freeze 3 hours or until firm.

6 Make espresso layer. Pour espresso layer over honey nougat layer in pan. Cover; freeze 3 hours, or overnight, until firm.

7 Stand semifreddo at room temperature 5 minutes before turning out. Remove lining paper. Serve topped with honeycomb.

ESPRESSO LAYER Beat egg yolks, extract, coffee and 2 tablespoons of the sugar in a small bowl with an electric mixer until thick and pale. Transfer mixture to a large bowl. Beat egg whites in a clean small bowl with an electric mixer until soft peaks form. Gradually add remaining sugar; beat until thick and glossy. Beat cream in another clean small bowl with electric mixer until soft peaks form. Fold egg whites and cream into egg yolk mixture.

RASPBERRY RICOTTA CHEESECAKE WITH AMARETTI CRUST

**PREP + COOK TIME 1 HOUR 30 MINUTES
(+ REFRIGERATION & COOLING) ◆ SERVES 8**

200g (6½ ounces) amaretti biscuits

2 tablespoons caster (superfine) sugar

75g (2½ ounces) butter, melted

125g (4 ounces) raspberries

2 tablespoons icing (confectioners') sugar

2 tablespoons water

150g (4½ ounces) raspberries, extra

2 teaspoons icing (confectioners') sugar, extra

RASPBERRY RICOTTA FILLING

500g (1 pound) cream cheese

300g (9½ ounces) ricotta

1 cup (220g) caster (superfine) sugar

⅓ cup (80ml) milk

3 eggs

125g (4 ounces) raspberries

1   Grease a 20cm (8-inch) springform pan. Line base and side with baking paper.

2   Process biscuits and caster sugar until fine. With motor operating, gradually add butter until well combined. Press biscuit mixture over base of tin using the back of a spoon. Place tin on an oven tray; refrigerate 30 minutes.

3   Preheat oven to 150°C/300°F.

4   Make raspberry ricotta filling; pour filling into pan.

5   Bake for 50 minutes or until cooked around the edge and slightly wobbly in the middle. Turn oven off; cool cheesecake in oven 1 hour with the door ajar. Refrigerate at least 4 hours or overnight, until firm.

6   Process raspberries, icing sugar and the water until pureed. Strain through a sieve into a small bowl. Spread puree over cheesecake, top with extra raspberries; dust with extra icing sugar.

RASPBERRY RICOTTA FILLING Process cheeses, sugar and milk until smooth. Add eggs; process until combined. Transfer mixture to a large bowl; fold in raspberries.

TEST KITCHEN NOTES

DEPENDING ON THE DESIGN OF THE SPRINGFORM PAN, CLIP THE BASE IN UPSIDE DOWN SO THE BASE IS LEVEL AND THE CHEESECAKE IS EASY TO REMOVE. THE TOP OF THE CHEESECAKE MAY CRACK SLIGHTLY ON COOLING BUT IT WILL BE COVERED BEFORE SERVING. USE THAWED FROZEN RASPBERRIES FOR THE RASPBERRY SAUCE.

AMARETTI ARE ITALIAN BISCUITS MADE FROM ALMONDS. THEY ARE AVAILABLE FROM DELICATESSENS AND SUPERMARKETS.

COCONUT PANNA COTTA WITH MANGO AND COCONUT WAFERS

PREP + COOK TIME 45 MINUTES (+ COOLING & REFRIGERATION) ◆ SERVES 6

300ml pouring cream

½ cup (110g) caster (superfine) sugar

2 teaspoons powdered gelatine

⅓ cup (80ml) boiling water

375g (12 ounces) Greek-style vanilla yoghurt

1 teaspoon coconut extract

COCONUT WAFERS

1 sheet puff pastry

1 egg white

½ cup (40g) desiccated coconut

CARAMELISED MANGOES

2 medium mangoes (860g)

⅓ cup (75g) caster (superfine) sugar

CARAMEL SAUCE

⅓ cup (75g) caster (superfine) sugar

⅓ cup (80ml) water

2 tablespoons lemon juice

1 Stir cream and sugar in a medium saucepan, over high heat, without boiling, until sugar dissolves. Sprinkle gelatine over the boiling water in a small heatproof jug, stand jug in a small saucepan of simmering water; stir until gelatine dissolves. Stir gelatine mixture into hot cream mixture. Transfer to a medium bowl; cool.

2 Stir yoghurt and extract into cooled cream mixture.

3 Rinse six ½-cup (125ml) moulds with cold water; drain, do not wipe dry. Pour yoghurt mixture into moulds, cover loosely with plastic wrap. Refrigerate 4 hours or until set.

4 Make coconut wafers and caramelised mangoes, then caramel sauce.

5 Carefully turn panna cotta onto serving plates, add caramelised mangoes; spoon over caramel sauce. Serve with coconut wafers.

COCONUT WAFERS Preheat oven to 200°C/400°F. Grease and line an oven tray with baking paper. Cut pastry in half, cut each half into four triangles; place on tray. Bake about 10 minutes. Remove from oven, brush with egg white, sprinkle with coconut. Bake a further 5 minutes or until coconut is golden.

CARAMELISED MANGOES Remove cheeks from mangoes; using a large metal spoon, scoop flesh from skin then cut in half lengthways. Sprinkle cut surfaces of mango with sugar. Heat a large frying pan; cook mango, cut-side down, for 2 minutes or until caramelised. Remove from pan; cool.

CARAMEL SAUCE Place sugar and 2 tablespoons of the water in a small heavy-based saucepan over medium heat; cook, swirling pan frequently, for 4 minutes or until deep golden. Add juice and the remaining water; swirl pan until combined and syrupy. Cool completely.

PASSIONFRUIT JELLY WITH POACHED PINEAPPLE

PREP + COOK TIME 35 MINUTES (+ REFRIGERATION) ♦ SERVES 6

12 passionfruit

¾ cup (180ml) fresh orange juice, strained

¼ cup (60ml) fresh lemon juice, strained

¾ cup (165g) caster (superfine) sugar

1 cup (250ml) water

1 tablespoon powdered gelatine

⅓ cup (80ml) boiling water

½ cup (40g) flaked coconut or shaved fresh coconut, toasted

POACHED PINEAPPLE

1 small pineapple (900g)

1 cup (220g) caster (superfine) sugar

1 cup (250ml) water

10cm (4-inch) stick fresh lemon grass (20g), halved lengthways

4 fresh kaffir lime leaves, crushed

1 Halve passionfruit; scoop pulp into a fine sieve over a 2-cup (500ml) measuring jug. Press to extract as much juice as possible. Discard seeds. Add orange and lemon juices to passionfruit juice; you should have 2 cups juice.

2 Place juice in a medium saucepan with sugar and the water; stir over high heat, without boiling, until sugar dissolves. Bring to the boil; remove from heat.

3 Sprinkle gelatine over the boiling water in a small heatproof jug. Stand jug in a small saucepan of simmering water; stir until gelatine dissolves. Stir gelatine mixture into juice mixture.

4 Pour mixture into six 1-cup (250ml) glasses. Cover; refrigerate 4 hours or until set.

5 Meanwhile, make poached pineapple.

6 Serve jellies topped with poached pineapple and coconut.

POACHED PINEAPPLE Peel pineapple; cut in half lengthways. Slice each half into very thin slices. Combine sugar and the water in a medium saucepan; stir over high heat, without boiling, until sugar dissolves. Add lemon grass to syrup with lime leaves; bring to the boil. Reduce heat; simmer, uncovered, about 5 minutes. Add pineapple; simmer, uncovered, for 3 minutes or until pineapple is tender. Transfer pineapple mixture to a medium heatproof bowl. Cover; refrigerate 2 hours.

TEST KITCHEN NOTES

TO TOAST THE COCONUT, STIR IN A MEDIUM FRYING PAN OVER LOW-MEDIUM HEAT FOR 3 MINUTES OR UNTIL GOLDEN. REMOVE COCONUT FROM PAN IMMEDIATELY TO PREVENT OVER-BROWNING.

FRESH
COCONUT
CAN BE SHAVED
USING A VEGETABLE
PEELER.

curry

curry powder a blend of ground spices used for convenience. Choose mild or hot to suit your taste.

green paste the hottest of the traditional pastes; contains chilli, garlic, onion, salt, lemon grass, spices and galangal.

tandoori paste a highly-seasoned classic East-Indian marinade flavoured with garlic, tamarind, ginger, coriander, chilli and other spices, and used to give foods the authentic red-orange tint of tandoor oven cooking.

tikka paste a medium-mild paste of chilli, coriander, cumin, lentil flour, garlic, ginger, turmeric, fennel, cloves, cinnamon and cardamom.

tom yum paste a Thai-style paste with a hot, spicy and sour flavour. Containing lemon grass, red chilli, sugar, onion, anchovy, galangal, kaffir lime and paprika. It is used to make the traditional spicy sour prawn soup known as tom yum goong.

dukkah an Egyptian spice blend made with roasted nuts and aromatic spices. It is available from Middle-Eastern food stores, specialty spice stores and some supermarkets.

eggplant also known as aubergine.

fennel also known as finocchio or anise; a white to very pale green-white, firm, crisp, roundish vegetable about 8-12cm in diameter. The bulb has a slightly sweet, anise flavour but the leaves have a much stronger taste. Also the name of dried seeds having a licorice flavour.

fish fillets, firm white blue eye, bream, flathead, swordfish, ling, whiting, jewfish, snapper or sea perch are all good choices. Check for small pieces of bone and use tweezers to remove them.

five-spice powder also known as chinese five-spice; a fragrant mixture of ground cinnamon, cloves, star anise, sichuan pepper and fennel seeds.

flour

plain (all-purpose) a general unbleached wheat flour, the best for baking: the gluten content ensures a strong dough, for a light result.

self-raising (self-rising) plain flour sifted with baking powder in the proportion of 1 cup flour to 2 teaspoons baking powder.

galangal a rhizome with a hot ginger-citrusy flavour; used similarly to ginger and garlic as a seasoning or an ingredient.

kaffir lime leaves also known as bai magrood. Aromatic leaves of a citrus tree; two glossy dark green leaves joined end to end, forming a rounded hourglass shape. A strip of fresh lime peel may be substituted for each kaffir lime leaf.

kumara the Polynesian name of an orange-fleshed sweet potato often confused with yam.

lebanese cucumber short, slender and thin-skinned. Probably the most popular variety because of its tender, edible skin, tiny, yielding seeds and sweet, fresh flavoursome taste.

leek a member of the onion family, the leek resembles a green onion but is much larger and more subtle in flavour. Tender baby or pencil leeks can be eaten whole with minimal cooking, but adult leeks are usually trimmed of most of the green tops then chopped or sliced.

lemon grass a tall, clumping, lemon-smelling and -tasting, sharp-edged grass; the white part of the stem is used, finely chopped, in cooking.

lentils (red, brown, yellow) dried pulses often identified by and named after their colour; also known as dhal.

mayonnaise we use whole-egg mayonnaise in our recipes.

mesclun a salad mix or gourmet salad mix with a mixture of assorted young lettuce and other green leaves, including baby spinach leaves, mizuna and curly endive.

mince also known as ground meat.

mirin a Japanese champagne-coloured cooking wine; made of glutinous rice and alcohol and used expressly for cooking. Should not be confused with sake.

mushrooms

enoki clumps of long, spaghetti-like stems with tiny, snowy white caps.

flat large, flat mushrooms with a rich earthy flavour. They are sometimes misnamed field mushrooms, which are wild mushrooms.

oyster also known as abalone; grey-white mushroom shaped like a fan. Prized for their smooth texture and subtle, oyster-like flavour.

shiitake when fresh are also known as chinese black, forest or golden oak mushrooms; although cultivated, they are large and meaty and have the earthiness and taste of wild mushrooms. When dried, they are known as donko or dried chinese mushrooms; rehydrate before use.

swiss brown also known as cremini or roman mushrooms; light brown mushrooms with a full-bodied flavour.

mustard seeds available in black, brown or yellow varieties. They are available from major supermarkets and health food shops.

noodles

bean thread vermicelli made from mung bean flour. Fine, delicate noodles also known as wun sen, cellophane or glass noodles (because they are transparent when cooked). Available dried in various-sized bundles. Must be soaked to soften before use.

egg, fresh also known as ba mee or yellow noodles. Made from wheat flour and eggs. Range in size from very fine strands to wide, thick spaghetti-like pieces as thick as a shoelace.

hokkien also known as stir-fry noodles; fresh wheat noodles resembling thick, yellow-brown spaghetti needing no pre-cooking.

ramen, fresh comes in various shapes and lengths. They may be fat, thin or even ribbon-like, as well as straight or wrinkled. While more often sold dried, fresh ramen is available from some Asian food stores. Substitute with reconstituted dried noodles.

rice vermicelli, dried very fine noodles made from rice flour and water, vermicelli is often compressed into blocks and dried. Before using, soak in boiling water until tender.

soba a thin spaghetti-like pale brown noodle from Japan; made from buckwheat and varying proportions of wheat flour.

onions

green also known as scallion or, incorrectly, shallot; an immature onion picked before the bulb has formed. Has a long, bright-green edible stalk.

red also known as spanish, red spanish or bermuda onion; a sweet-flavoured, large, purple-red onion.

shallots also called french shallots, golden shallots or eschalots; small, brown-skinned, elongated members of the onion family.

spring small white bulbs and long, narrow, green-leafed tops.

pak choy similar to baby buk choy, except the stem is a very pale green, rather than white, and the top is less leafy.

pappadums dried cracker-like wafers made from lentil and rice flours. If uncooked they must be reconstituted before they are eaten. We give them a burst in a microwave oven, but they are usually deep-fried to make them puff and double in size.

paprika ground, dried, sweet red capsicum (bell pepper); there are many types available, including sweet, hot, mild and smoked.

parsley, flat-leaf also known as continental or italian parsley.

pasta

farfalle a short, rather sturdy butterfly-shaped pasta that is also known as 'bow-ties'.

fusilli also known as 'corkscrews'. Dried spiral-shaped pasta.

rigatoni a form of tube-shaped pasta. it is larger than penne and is usually ridged, the end doesn't terminate at an angle, like penne does.

peppercorns

pink dried berry from a type of rose plant grown in Madagascar, usually sold packed in brine; they possess a distinctive pungently sweet taste.

sichuan also known as chinese pepper. Small, red-brown aromatic seeds resembling black peppercorns; they have a peppery-lemon flavour.

pitta also known as lebanese bread.

pizza bases pre-packaged for home-made pizzas. They come in a variety of sizes and thicknesses (thin and crispy or thick).

polenta also known as cornmeal; a flour-like cereal made of ground corn (maize). Also the name of the dish made from it.

preserved lemon rind a North African specialty; lemons are quartered and preserved in salt and lemon juice or water. To use, remove and discard pulp, squeeze juice from rind, rinse rind well; slice thinly. Refrigerate once opened.

prosciutto unsmoked italian ham; salted, air-cured and aged.

rice

arborio small, round grain rice well-suited to absorb a large amount of liquid; the high level of starch makes it especially suitable for risottos.

basmati a white, fragrant long-grained rice. Wash several times before cooking.

jasmine fragrant long-grained rice; white rice can be substituted, but will not taste the same.

medium grain previously sold as calrose rice; extremely versatile rice that can be substituted for short or long grain rices if necessary.

rocket also known as arugula, rugula and rucola; a peppery-tasting green leaf. Baby rocket leaves are smaller and less peppery.

sake made from fermented rice. If sake is unavailable, dry sherry, vermouth or brandy can be substituted. Cooking sake (containing salt) is also available.

sambal oelek (also ulek or olek) Indonesian in origin; a salty paste made from ground chillies and vinegar. Found in supermarkets and Asian food stores.

sauces

black bean a Chinese sauce made from fermented soya beans, spices, water and wheat flour.

char siu a Chinese barbecue sauce made from sugar, water, salt, fermented soya bean paste, honey, soy sauce, malt syrup and spices. It can be found at most supermarkets.

fish also called nam pla or nuoc nam; made from pulverised salted fermented fish, most often anchovies. Has a pungent smell and strong taste, so use sparingly.

hoisin a thick, sweet and spicy Chinese paste made from salted fermented soya beans, onions and garlic.

oyster Asian in origin, this rich, brown sauce is made from oysters and their brine, cooked with salt and soy sauce, and thickened with starches.

plum a thick, sweet and sour dipping sauce made from plums, vinegar, sugar, chillies and spices.

soy made from fermented soya beans. Several variations are available in most supermarkets and Asian food stores. We use japanese soy sauce unless otherwise indicated. It is the best table soy and the one to choose if you only want one type.

dark soy deep brown, almost black in colour; rich, with a thicker consistency than other types. Pungent but not that salty.

japanese soy an all-purpose low-sodium soy sauce made with more wheat content than its Chinese counterparts.

kecap manis (ketjap manis); a thick soy sauce with added sugar and spices. The sweetness is derived from the addition of molasses or palm sugar.

light soy a fairly thin, pale but salty tasting sauce; used in dishes in which the natural colour of the ingredients is to be maintained. Do not confuse with salt-reduced or low-sodium soy sauces.

sweet chilli a mild sauce made from red chillies, sugar, garlic and vinegar.

silver beet also known as swiss chard; mistakenly called spinach.

snow peas also called mange tout (eat all). Snow pea tendrils, the growing shoots of the plant, are also available at greengrocers.

snow pea sprouts the tender new growths of snow peas.

spinach also known as english spinach and, incorrectly, silver beet.

sugar

brown very soft, finely granulated sugar retaining molasses for its characteristic colour and flavour.

caster also known as superfine or finely granulated table sugar.

icing also known as confectioners' sugar or powdered sugar.

palm also known as nam tan pip, jaggery, jawa or gula melaka; made from the sap of the sugar palm tree. Light brown to black in colour and usually sold in rock-hard cakes; substitute with brown sugar if unavailable.

white a coarsely granulated table sugar, also known as crystal sugar.

sugar snap peas also known as honey snap peas; fresh small peas that can be eaten whole, pod and all, similarly to snow peas.

sumac a purple-red, astringent spice ground from berries growing on shrubs flourishing wild around the Mediterranean; adds a tart, lemony flavour to food. Available from spice shops and major supermarkets.

tahini a rich, sesame-seed paste, used in most Middle-Eastern cuisines.

tortilla thin, round unleavened bread made from wheat flour or corn.

turmeric related to ginger; adds a golden-yellow colour to food.

vinegar

balsamic originally from Modena, Italy, there are now many balsamic vinegars on the market ranging in pungency and quality depending on how long they have been aged. Is a deep rich brown colour and has a sweet and sour flavour. Quality can be determined up to a point by price; use the most expensive sparingly.

red wine based on fermented red wine.

rice a colourless vinegar made from fermented rice, sugar and salt. also known as seasoned rice vinegar.

white made from spirit of cane sugar.

white wine made from white wine.

vietnamese mint not a mint at all, but a pungent and peppery narrow-leafed member of the buckwheat family.

watercress one of the cress family, a large group of peppery greens. Highly perishable, so must be used as soon as possible after purchase.

wombok also known as napa, peking or chinese cabbage or petsai. Elongated in shape with pale green, crinkly leaves. This is the most common cabbage in South-East Asian cooking.

yoghurt, Greek-style often made from sheep milk that is strained in a cloth (traditionally muslin) to remove the whey and to give it a thick, smooth, creamy consistency, almost like whipped cream.

za'atar a Middle Eastern herb and spice mixture which varies in makeup; however, it always includes thyme, ground sumac and, usually, toasted sesame seeds.

zucchini also called courgette; a small, pale- or dark-green or yellow vegetable.

CONVERSION CHART

MEASURES

One Australian metric measuring cup holds approximately 250ml; one Australian metric tablespoon holds 20ml; one Australian metric teaspoon holds 5ml. The difference between one country's measuring cups and another's is within a two- or three-teaspoon variance, and will not affect your cooking results. North America, New Zealand and the United Kingdom use a 15ml tablespoon.

All cup and spoon measurements are level. The most accurate way of measuring dry ingredients is to weigh them. When measuring liquids, use a clear glass or plastic jug with the metric markings.

The imperial measurements used in these recipes are approximate only. Measurements for cake pans are approximate only. Using same-shaped cake pans of a similar size should not affect the outcome of your baking. We measure the inside top of the cake pan to determine sizes.

We use large eggs with an average weight of 60g.

DRY MEASURES

metric	imperial
15g	½oz
30g	1oz
60g	2oz
90g	3oz
125g	4oz (¼lb)
155g	5oz
185g	6oz
220g	7oz
250g	8oz (½lb)
280g	9oz
315g	10oz
345g	11oz
375g	12oz (¾lb)
410g	13oz
440g	14oz
470g	15oz
500g	16oz (1lb)
750g	24oz (1½lb)
1kg	32oz (2lb)

LIQUID MEASURES

metric	imperial
30ml	1 fluid oz
60ml	2 fluid oz
100ml	3 fluid oz
125ml	4 fluid oz
150ml	5 fluid oz
190ml	6 fluid oz
250ml	8 fluid oz
300ml	10 fluid oz
500ml	16 fluid oz
600ml	20 fluid oz
1000ml (1 litre)	1¾ pints

LENGTH MEASURES

metric	imperial
3mm	⅛ in
6mm	¼in
1cm	½in
2cm	¾in
2.5cm	1in
5cm	2in
6cm	2½in
8cm	3in
10cm	4in
13cm	5in
15cm	6in
18cm	7in
20cm	8in
22cm	9in
25cm	10in
28cm	11in
30cm	12in (1ft)

OVEN TEMPERATURES

The oven temperatures in this book are for conventional ovens; if you have a fan-forced oven, decrease the temperature by 10-20 degrees.

	°C (CELSIUS)	°F (FAHRENHEIT)
Very slow	120	250
Slow	150	300
Moderately slow	160	325
Moderate	180	350
Moderately hot	200	400
Hot	220	425
Very hot	240	475

INDEX